Long-term positive, optimistic thinking.

Book content:

PROLOGUE

Long term positive, optimistic thinking help us:

I. To accomplish:

      1. More successes

      2. Bigger successes

      3. More perosnal objectives

      4. Mentain a happy marriage

      5. More of what we want

      6. Etc.

II.   To prevent more:

      1. Failures

      2. Errors

      3. Accidents

      4. Unfavorable situations

      5. Etc.

III. Be more:

      1. Happy

      2. Optimistic

3. Confident in our capabilities
4. Confident in the achievemt of personal objectives
5. Confident in accomplishing of what we want
6. Etc.

IV. Use more efficiently:

1. Time
2. Financial resources
3. Material resources
4. Belongings
5. Experience
6. Knowledge
7. Etc.

V. Become much more:

1. Strong
2. Efficient
3. Productives
4. Confident in the achivement of personal objectives
5. Sure of life success

6. Etc.

The ideas about the long term positive, creative, optimistic, preventive thinking are indispensable in accomplishing personal objectives and of all that we want in life.

The money invested in this book of mine and the others that follow it is worth it, and it is almost nothing comparing to the pozitive efects that this book can have in your life, by applying the ideas to your life.

This volumes must be bought and used day by day, in order to development your personality and to the accomplish of all that you want.

These books contain lots of pozitive, optimist, creative, dinamic ideas, that push you to action, to thinking, things that are necesary your daily life and to accomplish your personal objectives.

Reading and analizing the ideas in this book and aplying them, we'll fiind solutions and ideas that will help us find:

I. To discover:

1. Qualities

2. Defects

3. Capabilities

4. Qualifications

5. Some opportunities to succeed in life

6. Feelings

7. What we do to be loved

8. How to love

9. how to realize and maintain a true mutual love

10. How to realize and maintain a happy marriage

11. Mistakes, errors, wrong ideas

12. Etc.

II. To prevent some:

1. Divorces

2. Mistakes

3. Suspect

4. Griefs

5. Conflicts

6. Accidents

7. Failures

8. Bankrupstcy

9. Etc.

III. To become more:

1. Happy
2. Loved
3. Honored,
4. Appreciated,
5. Wanted,
6. Optimistic,
7. Ggood,
8. Unselfish,
9. Emotional,
10. Altruists
11. Stronger
12. Efficient
13. Organized
14. Planners
15. Active
16. Honest
17. Human
18. Popular
19. Famous

20. Flexible

21. Adaptable

22. Understanding

23. Prompt

24. Etc.

IV. To get out of a state of:

1. Despair

2. Pessimism

3. Passiveness

4. Inactivity

5. Inefficiency

6. Inflexibility

7. Crisis

8. Inadaptability

9. Etc.

V. To participate more actively to:

1. Social life

2. Political life

3. Nonprofit organizations activities

4. Etc.

VI.   To participate more actively and efficiently in achieving true love and a happy marriage

VII.   To find more likely situations conducive to achieving and maintaining a happy marriage life

VIII.   To change our life for the better and to make it more beautiful

IX.   To multiply and increase the chances to find your life partner

X.   To raise and educate our children better so we can take better care of them.

XI.   Fiind more and bigger chances to meet favourable situations to accomplish and maintain a happy marriage for life.

XII.   Change our life in good and make it better.

XIII.   To multiply and increase the chances to find your life partner

XIV.   To raise and educate our children better so we can take better care of them.

I write and gather these thoughts, ideas in books, internet and other publications because these are useful to us every day and it is necessary to apply them to accomplish what we want, a better and beautiful life and propsperous.

These thoughts reflect a small part of what is good in reality and human relationships.

I wait to hear from you good news, good deeds that you have done influenced from what you have read from these books to make your life more beautiful, properous, happier and to be a pozitive example for others.

Each of us an become pozitive examples for others around us, participating to the creation of a better, prosperous and happier human society.

I'd be happy if one or more ideas read from these books helped you in a way or another and made you happier and prosperous.

I'm waiting to hear from you, your ideas and oppinions, your joys and griefes and your suggestions for new book subjects and i also appeal to your participation of promoting on the internet and mass media of the ideas and the books i've written.

I invite you to e-mail me at my email address: agcornel@gmail.com.

Dear readers I wish you all health, happiness and achievement of all your wishes.

Best regards and respect,

Gheorghe Cornel Ardelean
981 Principal Street
Macea, Arad county
Zip Code 371210
Romania
Tel # (40)-0788-725-204
(40)-0788-725-913

Accomplish

1. The ability of accomplishing records helps us achieve more performances.

2. The desire to accomplish positive deeds helps us achieve more performances.

3. The ability of accomplishing records helps us achieve much good luck.

4. The power used to accomplish positive deeds helps us achieve more favorable chances.

5. The desire to accomplish positive deeds helps us achieve more records.

6. The desire to accomplish positive deeds helps us achieve more favorable chances.

7. The power used to accomplish positive deeds helps us achieve more pleasant surprises.

8. The passion of accomplishing successes helps us achieve more efficient co operations.

9. The power used to accomplish positive deeds helps us achieve more successes.

10. The power used to accomplish positive deeds helps us achieve more personal goals.

11. The desire to accomplish positive deeds helps us achieve more true friendships.

12. The ability to accomplish personal objectives helps us achieve more efficient co operations.

13. The ability of accomplishing records helps us achieve more efficient co operations.

14. The desire to accomplish records helps us achieve more personal goals.

15. The desire to accomplish records helps us achieve more favorable chances.

16. The passion of accomplishing successes helps us achieve more successes.

17. The desire to accomplish records helps us achieve much good luck.

18. The desire to accomplish records helps us achieve more successes.

19. The desire to accomplish positive deeds helps us achieve more personal goals.

20.   The ability to accomplish personal objectives helps us achieve more true friendships.

21.   The power used to accomplish positive deeds helps us achieve more efficient co operations.

22.   The desire to accomplish positive deeds helps us achieve much good luck.

23.   The passion of accomplishing successes helps us achieve more favorable chances.

24.   The passion of accomplishing successes helps us achieve more personal goals.

25.   The ability of accomplishing records helps us achieve more records.

26.   The passion of accomplishing successes helps us achieve much good luck.

27.   The ability to accomplish personal objectives helps us achieve more favorable situations.

28.   The desire to accomplish records helps us achieve more performances.

29.   The power used to accomplish positive deeds helps us achieve much good luck.

30. The passion of accomplishing successes helps us achieve more pleasant surprises.

31. The power used to accomplish positive deeds helps us achieve more performances.

32. The ability of accomplishing records helps us achieve more favorable chances.

33. The desire to accomplish records helps us achieve more records.

34. The desire to accomplish records helps us achieve more true friendships.

35. he desire to accomplish records helps us achieve more pleasant surprises.

36. The ability of accomplishing records helps us achieve more favorable situations.

37. The passion of accomplishing successes helps us achieve more performances.

38. The ability of accomplishing records helps us achieve more successes.

39. The ability to accomplish personal objectives helps us achieve more pleasant surprises.

40. The ability to accomplish personal objectives helps us achieve more personal goals.

41. The power used to accomplish positive deeds helps us achieve more favorable situations.

42. The ability of accomplishing records helps us achieve more pleasant surprises.

43. The ability of accomplishing records helps us achieve more true friendships.

44. The ability to accomplish personal objectives helps us achieve more favorable chances.

45. The passion of accomplishing successes helps us achieve more true friendships.

46. The desire to accomplish positive deeds helps us achieve more efficient co operations.

47. The desire to accomplish positive deeds helps us achieve more favorable situations.

48. The power used to accomplish positive deeds helps us achieve more records.

49. The desire to accomplish records helps us achieve more favorable situations.

Achieve

50. The ability of achieving performances helps us achieve more successes.

51. Openness towards new efficient actions helps us achieve much good luck.

52. The desire to want more helps us achieve more favorable situations.

53. Finding creative solutions that contribute to solving conflicts helps us achieve more records.

54. Hiring the best people helps us achieve much good luck.

55. The loyalty of friends helps us achieve much good luck.

56. Preventing conflicts helps us achieve more personal goals.

57. Learning from other people's mistakes helps us achieve more favorable situations.

58. The power of continuously being effective helps us achieve more personal goals.

59. The desire to achieve successes helps us achieve more pleasant surprises.

60. Permanent concentration on our personal objectives helps us achieve more efficient co operations.

61. Not being concerned about what others might think of us helps us achieve more favorable situations.

62. Preventing everything that harms women helps us achieve more true friendships.

63. Taking work seriously helps us achieve more records.

64. Preventing the inefficient use of the resources of informatics helps us achieve more efficient co operations.

65. The ability of accomplishing records helps us achieve more performances.

66. Team spirit helps us achieve more records.

67. Preventing accidents helps us achieve more true friendships.

68. Discovering true passion helps us achieve more favorable situations.

69. The desire to achieve successes helps us achieve more favorable chances.

70. The passion of achieving personal goals helps us achieve more efficient co operations.

71. Prevention against bad people helps us achieve more personal goals.

72. The desire to accomplish positive deeds helps us achieve more performances.

73. Preventing everything that harms children helps us achieve more favorable situations.

74. Preventing everything that harms women helps us achieve more records.

75. Preventing negative facts helps us achieve more favorable chances.

76. Assuming initiatives helps us achieve much good luck.

77. Openness towards new solutions helps us achieve more successes.

78. Preventing the inefficient use of financial resources helps us achieve much good luck.

79. The daily gathering of as much experience as possible helps us achieve more pleasant surprises.

80. The great capacity of taking efficient decisions helps us achieve more efficient co operations.

81. Finding creative solutions to the problems helps us achieve more true friendships.

82. The power of persevering helps us achieve much good luck.

83. Effective daily actions that are completed with passion help us achieve more successes.

84. Using adverse events in our favor helps us achieve more successes.

85. Team spirit helps us achieve more favorable chances.

86. Useful ideas help us achieve more pleasant surprises.

87. The desire of achieving good deeds helps us achieve more performances.

88. The desire to be better helps us achieve more efficient co operations.

89. Rising from more failures helps us achieve more efficient co operations.

90. The art of solving arguments helps us achieve more true friendships.

91. Openness towards new solutions helps us achieve more true friendships.

92. Imitating positive deeds helps us achieve more favorable situations.

93. The desire to be better helps us achieve more successes.

94. The desire to become even more effective helps us achieve more personal goals.

95. Openness towards new ideas helps us achieve more favorable situations.

96. The power of not allowing ourselves to be stopped helps us achieve more pleasant surprises.

97. The ability of accomplishing records helps us achieve much good luck.

98. Useful ideas help us achieve more efficient co operations.

99. Preventing conflicts helps us achieve more favorable chances.

Accomplishments

100. We can contribute to the achievement of our greatest accomplishments also through the contribution of the formation, development, maintenance and usage of inventive behavior.

101. We can contribute to the achievement of our greatest accomplishments also through the contribution of the formation, development, maintenance and usage of continuous self-motivating behavior.

102. We can contribute to the achievement of our greatest accomplishments also through the contribution of the formation, development, maintenance and usage of expansive behavior.

103. We can contribute to the achievement of our greatest accomplishments also through the contribution of the formation, development, maintenance and usage of sociable behavior.

104. We can contribute to the achievement of our greatest accomplishments also through the contribution of the formation, development,

maintenance and usage of unpretentious behavior.

105. We can contribute to the achievement of our greatest accomplishments also through the contribution of the formation, development, maintenance and usage of profound behavior.

106. We can contribute to the achievement of our greatest accomplishments also through the contribution of the formation, development, maintenance and usage of being an efficient negotiator behavior.

107. We can contribute to the achievement of our greatest accomplishments also through the contribution of the formation, development, maintenance and usage of peaceful behavior.

108. We can contribute to the achievement of our greatest accomplishments also through the contribution of the formation, development, maintenance and usage of a behavior of being in love with life.

109. We can contribute to the achievement of our greatest accomplishments also through the contribution of the formation, development,

maintenance and usage of animated behavior.

110. We can contribute to the achievement of our greatest accomplishments also through the contribution of the formation, development, maintenance and usage of consequent behavior.

111. We can contribute to the achievement of our greatest accomplishments also through the contribution of the formation, development, maintenance and usage of diligent behavior.

112. We can contribute to the achievement of our greatest accomplishments also through the contribution of the formation, development, maintenance and usage of receptive to new behavior.

113. We can contribute to the achievement of our greatest accomplishments also through the contribution of the formation, development, maintenance and usage of sportive behavior. We can contribute to the achievement of our greatest accomplishments also through the contribution of the formation, development, maintenance and usage of firm behavior.

114. We can contribute to the achievement of our greatest accomplishments also through the contribution of the formation, development, maintenance and usage of initiating behavior.

115. We can contribute to the achievement of our greatest accomplishments also through the contribution of the formation, development, maintenance and usage of conscientious behavior.

Adaptability

116. In order to transform positive objectives into reality it is necessary to form, develop, maintain and use the sense of adaptability.

117. The limits we have set can be overcome by the formation, development, maintenance and usage of the sense of adaptability.

118. In order to change our life it is necessary to form, develop, maintain and use the sense of adaptability.

119. Our transformation for the better can be achieved also through the contribution of the

formation, development, maintenance and usage of adaptability to each situation.

120. People who have not succeeded in obtaining a happy marriage must develop their sense of adaptability.

121. Those who have high objectives in life mostly have the sense of adaptability.

Actions

122. Openness towards new efficient actions helps us achieve much good luck.

123. Effective daily actions that are completed with passion help us achieve more successes.

124. Our everyday effective actions help us achieve more efficient co operations.

125. Effective daily actions that are completed with passion help us achieve more favorable chances.

126. Our everyday effective actions help us achieve more successes.

127. Imitating efficient actions helps us achieve more performances.

128. Our everyday effective actions help us achieve more pleasant surprises.

129. Imitating efficient actions helps us achieve much good luck.

130. Openness towards new efficient actions helps us achieve more performances.

131. Our everyday effective actions help us achieve more personal goals.

132. Our everyday effective actions help us achieve more favorable situations.

133. Openness towards new efficient actions helps us achieve more favorable chances.

134. Our everyday effective actions help us achieve more performances.

135. Imitating efficient actions helps us achieve more favorable chances.

136. Openness towards new efficient actions helps us achieve more true friendships.

137. Imitating efficient actions helps us achieve more successes.

138. Imitating efficient actions helps us achieve more efficient co operations.

139. Imitating efficient actions helps us achieve more pleasant surprises.

140. Effective daily actions that are completed with passion help us achieve much good luck.

141. Imitating efficient actions helps us achieve more true friendships.

142. Our everyday effective actions help us achieve more true friendships.

143. Effective daily actions that are completed with passion help us achieve more efficient co operations.

144. Openness towards new efficient actions helps us achieve more favorable situations.

145. Openness towards new efficient actions helps us achieve more successes.

146. Openness towards new efficient actions helps us achieve more records.

147. Imitating efficient actions helps us achieve more records.

148. Openness towards new efficient actions helps us achieve more efficient co operations.

149. Openness towards new efficient actions helps us achieve more pleasant surprises.

150. Effective daily actions that are completed with passion help us achieve more pleasant surprises.

151. Our everyday effective actions help us achieve more favorable chances.

152. Our everyday effective actions help us achieve more records.

153. Effective daily actions that are completed with passion help us achieve more performances.

154. Effective daily actions that are completed with passion help us achieve more records.

155. Imitating efficient actions helps us achieve more favorable situations.

156. Effective daily actions that are completed with passion help us achieve more personal goals.

157. Effective daily actions that are completed with passion help us achieve more favorable situations.

158. Our everyday effective actions help us achieve much good luck.

159. Effective daily actions that are completed with passion help us achieve more true friendships.

160. Openness towards new efficient actions helps us achieve more personal goals.

161. By developing their inner beauty, women also develop their abilities that can create satisfactions.

162. Our chances of becoming happy increase if we plan our actions correctly.

163. The self-control of our behaviors helps us a lot to prevent negative actions.

164. Successes in life can also be achieved thanks to efficiently planning our actions.

165. The actions of prevention of human errors must be encouraged.

166. The actions of prevention of human errors must be respected.

167. The actions of prevention of human errors must be promoted.

168. The actions of prevention of human errors must be supported.

169. The actions of prevention of human errors must be learned.

170. We can achieve a happy life only through positive effective actions.

171. Effective co operations and developments are due to very positive effective actions.

172. It is necessary for children to learn continuously, day by day, only positive effective actions.

173. Positive effective actions are those that carry out personal objectives.

174. Positive effective actions maintain a happy marriage.

175. Success is obtained only with positive effective actions.

Activities

176. Skill must be developed continuously in the activities we achieve.

177. In order to pursue and transform our personal goals into reality we need to form, develop, maintain and use the ability to be cooperative in the activities that we have.

178. Those who have high objectives in life are mostly people who are used to carry out the activities they have started.

179. Those who have high objectives in life are cooperative in activities.

180. In order to trace and transform our personal goals into reality it is necessary to form, develop, maintain and use the ability to be cooperative in the activities we have.

181. Obstacles that stop us from achieving our personal goals can be overcome also through the contribution of the formation, development, maintenance and usage of the ability to be cooperative in activities.

182. A cooperative man in activities achieves more efficient co operations.

183.	People who are used to carry out the activities they have started have the ability to achieve a happy marriage.

184.	People who are used to carry out the activities they have started more easily maintain true friendships.

185.	People who are used to carry out the activities they have started are reliable people.

186.	People who are used to carry out the activities they have started must be appreciated, promoted, supported and rewarded.

187.	People who are used to carry out the activities they have started contribute a lot in achieving the greater good.

188.	People who are used to carrying out the activities they have started have the possibility to become happy.

189.	People who are used to carry out the activities they have started have the possibility to become happy.

190. People who are used to carry out the activities they have started will succeed in life.

191. A competent man is an engine of progress in all areas of activities where he's competent.

192. A cooperative man in activities has much more chances to achieve true friendships.

193. People who are used to carrying out the activities they have started are those who have achieved outstanding performances.

194. People who are used to carrying out the activities they have started more easily and surely maintain a mature love.

195. People who are used to carrying out the activities they have started more easily achieve true friendships.

196. A man who cooperates in activities has much more chances to achieve a more beautiful life.

197. A cooperative man in activities has a greater potential to achieve more and greater successes.

198. A cooperative man in activities more easily achieves efficient co-developments.

199. A cooperative man in activities is more available to the exchange of information.

200. A cooperative man in activities has a greater potential of achieving his personal goals.

201. A cooperative man in activities has more possibilities of achieving more social relations.

202. Global co operations need to be in all areas of activities that they can be achieved in.

203. Humanist economy will continuously ensure workplaces and useful activities that are positive for all persons on the planet and it will eliminate and prevent unemployment.

204. Most people realize facts, activities a lot harder than they achieve a happy marriage.

205. Those who control circumstances are engines of progress in all areas of activities.

206. People who finished the activities they started have a very high chance to contribute to global humanization.

207. People who finish the activities they started are more credible.

208. A man who is cooperative during activities has more chances to participate in efficient global co operations.

209. A man who is cooperative during activities must be promoted, supported and rewarded.

210. Efficient global co operations will form and develop many local activities in many places of the world.

211. The production of ideas is one of the most efficient human activities.

212. A good state of health is an engine to achieving progress in all areas of activities.

213. People who succeed in carrying out the activities they had started have the capacity to achieve a more beautiful life.

214. People who succeed in carrying out the activities they had started have greater chances to meet favorable situations.

215. People who are cooperative in activities can contribute a lot to global humanization.

216. People who are used to carrying out the activities they had started have a high capacity to achieve a happy life.

217. People who are used to carrying out the activities they had started have a high capacity to prevent many failures.

218. People who are used to carrying out the activities they had started have greater chances to achieve more and greater successes.

219. People who are used to carrying out the activities they had started are the engines of progress in all fields of activity.

220. People who are used to carrying out the activities they had started have a high potential to achieve their desired future.

221. Working in teams of people with similar values is an engine of progress in common activities.

222. The man who is cooperative in activities has greater chances to prevent more failures.

223. In all countries the number and quality of non-profit organizations activities must increase greatly and continuously as they can contribute greatly to the development of

many problems in each country and in the world.

Adaptation

224. Our ability of optimal adaptation helps us achieve more efficient co operations.

225. The ability of optimal adaptation very much increases our possibility to achieve more true friendships.

226. The ability of optimal adaptation increases our possibilities maintain a happy marriage.

227. The desire to make others happy can be accomplished through the contribution of the formation, development, maintenance and usage of the sense of adaptation.

228. Adaptation helps us achieve more successes.

229. Adaptation helps us maintain happiness.

230. Adaptation must be a model.

231. Adaptation helps us become more loving.

232. Adaptation helps us achieve a happy marriage.

233. Adaptation helps us become tolerant.

234. Adaptation helps us maintain the way of being loving.

235. Adaptation helps us maintain the way of being understanding.

236. Adaptation helps us become more humane.

237. Adaptation must be appreciated.

238. Adaptation helps us achieve more true friendships.

239. Adaptation helps us maintain efficiency.

Adverse

240. Using adverse events in our favor helps us achieve more successes.

241. Using adverse events in our favor helps us achieve much good luck.

242. Using adverse events in our favor helps us achieve more performances.

243. Using adverse events in our favor helps us achieve more true friendships.

244. Using adverse events in our favor helps us achieve more personal goals.

245. Using adverse events in our favor helps us achieve more efficient co operations.

246. Using adverse events in our favor helps us achieve more pleasant surprises.

247. Using adverse events in our favor helps us achieve more favorable situations.

248. Using adverse events in our favor helps us achieve more records.

249. Using adverse events in our favor helps us achieve more favorable chances.

250. Preventing premature actions helps us a lot more to prevent actions that adversely affect us and the others.

251. Discrimination very much adversely affects the harmonious development of the personality of many children of the world's states.

252. The depression of one of the spouses sometimes adversely affects family relationships.

253. Some say that the greatest treasure of all is love. Love is a great treasure, which also makes other treasures greater ones or simply creates treasures. Indeed there are situations, moments in which love for us is the greatest treasure, however we can not generalize that this is the greatest treasure of life automatically. If we can look deeply in a general way we can not practically determine which the greatest treasure is. For example, our wisdom can be evaluated as the largest treasure for many reasons. Usually the wise manage to achieve true love and retain it. Without wisdom is very difficult to make and keep a true love. When wisdom disappears or the wise makes big mistakes that adversely affects love very much, or sometimes even destroys it can be seen what a great treasure wisdom is and how much love depends on wisdom.

254. A smaller or bigger number of people who at a certain time need protection varies a lot according to many causes. Causes that can make people need protection from society are very many and they can not be controlled by single individuals. They are

some unpredictable causes that adversely affect some individuals who can not cope with some individuals. It is necessary and imperative that society always has institutions and an objective to ensure effective and not formal protection of those who need it.

Advice

255. True friends give one another advice.

256. States need to create material, financial, legal, time conditions required by parents to educate, advice, consult, raise their children properly, to develop their harmonious personality.

257. We must not reject positive advice.

258. Wise advice is always needed.

259. Those who will consider positive pieces of advice will have more chances to achieve more performances.

260. Those who will consider wise advice will grow a more harmonious personality.

261. Those who will consider wise advice, will have much greater opportunities to achieve success.

262. Some of those who will consider wise advice will be sure to have riches.

263. Each of us continuously needs wise advice.

264. Those who will consider wise pieces of advice will have more chances of success.

Brave

265. A great capacity of being brave helps us maintain our productivity.

266. A great capacity of being brave helps us become more enthusiastic.

267. A great capacity of being brave helps us become happy.

268. Pessimism can be removed and replaced with optimism also through the contribution of the formation, development, maintenance and usage of brave behavior.

269. A great capacity of being brave helps us become more efficient.

270. Problems cannot be solved by the ideas that created them but also through the contribution of the formation, development, maintenance and usage of brave behavior.

271. A great capacity of being brave must be appreciated.

272. A great capacity of being brave helps us become efficient.

273. A great capacity of being brave helps us become wise.

274. We can overcome the difficulties that we must overcome also through the help of the formation, development, maintenance and usage of brave behavior.

275. Our future can be projected and achieved also through the contribution of the formation, development, maintenance and usage of brave behavior.

276. A great capacity of being brave helps us maintain our way of being loved.

277. Our happiness depends a lot also on the formation, development, maintenance and usage of brave behavior.

278. A great capacity of being brave helps us maintain our wisdom.

279. A great capacity of being brave must be maintained.

280. A great capacity of being brave helps us become cautious.

281. Hopes can be created also through the contribution of the formation, development, maintenance and usage of brave behavior.

Behave

282. In life, we must not behave like x or y says, but according to the way we think it is best, positive, correct, legal and human.

283. When the husband behaves badly with his wife and hates her, he alienates her from him.

284. Patience and the art of behaving patient is part of our wisdom. It is necessary to

continuously develop the capacity to endure and the art to behave with patience.

285. If some men would behave properly with women, there would be much less divorces and unhappy marriages in the world.

Beliefs

286. The strength of going against everybody's beliefs helps us achieve much good luck.

287. The strength of going against everybody's beliefs helps us achieve more successes.

288. The will of going against everyone else's beliefs helps us achieve more pleasant surprises.

289. The will of going against everyone else's beliefs helps us achieve more favorable situations.

290. The strength of going against everybody's beliefs helps us achieve more records.

291. Some successes are the effects of beliefs.

292. The strength of going against everybody's beliefs helps us achieve more true friendships.

293. Many problems can be avoided by the beliefs that we have.

Believe

294. Positive imagination can help us achieve more therefore we can believe that we are able to achieve more.

295. People who have had successes in life have mostly believed in their success.

296. People who have had successes in life have mostly believed in people.

297. When we believe in certain values we feel happy.

298. Those who believe that others are to blame for their mistakes are illogical in that rationality.

299. People who help others, most of the times help them because they believe it is good and necessary and not obligatory.

300. Fatigue can be prevented through the proper nutrition of the person concerned, through education, positive behavior, balanced life, intellectual exercises, perseverance, willpower, exercise, a value system that we believe in and that we respect, business dynamism, social relations, friends, mature love, a happy marriage, adequate rest when necessary, proper sleep, entertainment, etc..

301. Good mood can be achieved if the person concerned has adequate nourishment, it can be achieved through education, intellectual work, perseverance, willpower, exercise, a value system that we believe in and that we respect, business dynamism, social relationships, friends, mature love and a happy marriage.

302. Good humor can be maintained through a balanced life, a proper diet, education, intellectual exercises, psychical balance, perseverance, women, physical exercises, a value system in which we believe in and that we respect, positive activities, dynamism, social relations, friends, mature love, a happy marriage, etc.

303. Some who believe they are cool and who demand unconditional respect do not have at least common some sense in many situations.

304. Some lawyers, many believe it, have participated actively and passively to the achievement of many injustices, illegalities of their clients, worldwide, in almost all the countries of the world.

305. Some judges, unfortunately believe they are slave owners and do many wrong things, and those whose causes they judge are their slaves.

306. Sometimes unpleasant surprises appear just when you do not believe it.

307. Weariness can be prevented through proper diet, education, positive behavior balanced intellectual exercise, perseverance, will, exercise, a value system that we believe in and that we respect, business dynamism, social relations, friends, mature love, a happy marriage, adequate rest when necessary, appropriate sleep, entertainment, etc.

Calm

308.   Pessimism can be removed and replaced with optimism also through the contribution of the formation, development, maintenance and usage of calm behavior.

309.   Our own happiness can be achieved and maintained also through the contribution of the formation, development, maintenance and usage of calm behavior.

310.   Positive experience can be achieved also through the contribution of the formation, development, maintenance and usage of calm behavior.

311.   The force of our ideas can be augmented also through the contribution of the formation, development, maintenance and usage of calm behavior.

312.   In order to prevent not achieving our personal goals, it is necessary to also form, develop, maintain and use our calm behavior.

313.   Aspiring towards a more meaningful life can also be achieved through the formation, development, maintenance and usage of calm behavior.

314.	Our resistance to changing for the better can be overcome also through the contribution of the formation, development, maintenance and usage of calm behavior.

315.	We can prevent the falling apart of a happy marriage also through the contribution of the formation, development, maintenance and usage of calm behavior.

316.	Hopes can be created also through the contribution of the formation, development, maintenance and usage of calm behavior.

317.	We can overcome the difficulties that we must overcome also through the help of the formation, development, maintenance and usage of calm behavior.

318.	We can become stronger and we can not allow ourselves to be influenced by the world also through the contribution of the formation, development, maintenance and usage of calm behavior.

319.	In achieving our successes a contribution is also brought by the formation, development, maintenance and usage of calm behavior.

320. We can contribute to the achievement of our greatest accomplishments also through the contribution of the formation, development, maintenance and usage of calm behavior.

Capabilities

321. Each of us has had one or more bigger or smaller failures. It's good not to have any failures or as few failures as possible. Some or more failures could harm us very much. Those who were careful did not achieve failure or failures and have made smaller, fewer ones. Prevision helps us prevent many failures. The more experienced in previsioning we are, the greater ability we have to provide, as we have more knowledge necessary to achieve previsions etc.. the more we can make accurate previsions, prevent many mistakes, failures, trouble, accidents, conflicts, arguments, unsuccessful actions, etc. In our personal and professional life, it is necessary to continuously develop and to have that personal goal to develop to a maximum capacity the prevision in private life, the ability to use previsions. We can continuously increase the capacity of our prevision very much, as we live if we have

personal objectives, as we expand our ability to prevision and whether we act to continuously and effectively achieve this objective. Those who aimed at personal living as to develop the capacity of prevision continuously and concretely act with dedication to achieve their capacity to make a prevision which will help them achieve one or more very big successes, they will succeed to prevent many failures, troubles, etc., they will be able to achieve much in life, to have many happy, satisfying moments and so much happiness. The more we have a capacity of more than prevision, a more accurate, more efficient one, the more valuable we are for having this treasure. This treasure we can continuously increase greatly. The capacity of prevision generally contains more capacities of prevision in some actions, behaviors in the achievement of personal objectives, private, professional, specific ones, etc. It is necessary to develop those capabilities specific to prediction that we need. Knowledge, experience, qualifications, skills, etc., in a specific prevision capacity can be used to a greater or lesser degree in other capacities specific to prevision. The capacities of prevision are very necessary and very useful to us but unfortunately very few people have personal goals in life to continuously develop the specific performance of prevision. Due to the special importance of the capacity of prevision it is necessary and required to create and develop the science of the development of the capacity of prevision, because having this science we would have it by applying enormous positive effects on countless people that should develop and apply it indirectly on other people. The state would accelerate progress in many fields, would accelerate the reduction of illiteracy, poverty, illness, divorces out of arguments and conflict, accidents, what harms humans, animals, the environment, etc.. It would lead to solving many personal and state targets, it would create enormously many joys, much satisfaction and happiness. It would lead to the situation that most people no longer live at the whim of chance, with no personal, professional security, etc.. but on the contrary they would lead to more people having them as an objective and as they continue to live, they would develop the personal capacities necessary for their prevision and apply them every day, both in the establishment of private personal or professional life, it would be something concrete that will help them achieve more harmonious lives to achieve what they want and need for their families. There is the capacity of prevision in specific persons, specific societies, specific legal entities, nonprofit organizations, companies, banks, groups, collectivities, international and intergovernmental organizations. Both individuals and legal entities, must not live from hand to mouth, must act firmly, must study and evaluate the effects of positive and negative actions, decisions, etc. their objectives are also necessary to be: 1) to aim at continuing to develop their capacities of specific prediction that they need, 2) to apply, continuous use in any action, situation-specific prediction capabilities necessary and useful efforts, energy consumption and costs for the development and capacity of specific prevision that they need.

Failures can happen in each of our actions or less often. Our failures can be created by factors and actions sometimes difficult to identify and prevent. However there are actions where we can know all the factors that can create failures. Knowing the factors that create failures in actions, we can take the necessary measures to prevent them by reaching in some cases to zero failures, as they have succeeded in situations in a long time, in many states, especially people in the most developed countries of the world. How to develop more this science with the more than we can know more of the factors that could cause failures in certain situations to certain actions. Scientific knowledge can contribute greatly to preventing many failures in many actions. At present people do not use scientific knowledge, the human experience gained in books, studies, on the Internet, although they have committed enormously many failures, mistakes, although they could prevent many huge mistakes, failures if they would use efficient, organized, timely human experience and knowledge from books, the Internet when they would need it. Countries should take immediate measures and be more interested in people and use them when they need knowledge and human experience that can reach and can be used. Human knowledge is growing and increases daily awfully much, and human experience which can create the situation so that we can prevent every day more even more mistakes and failures with positive effects on our high society, to accelerate progress in many areas. Where we have failures we should never discourage and lose our wits, our balance inside, our optimism, morale or to start to grieve. If we do this, it would solve absolutely no problem, but on the contrary, it would stress us illogically, abnormally without any positive effects. Those who have achieved many successes knew how to cope with failure, learning from failures, to reduce the negative effects of failures. Many failures rather than strengthening us, they weaken us, they should give us power instead of imobilizing us and mobilize us instead of making them harder to give motivation, instead of multiple negative effects they should have have multiple positive effects.

However, I disagree and do not consider as logical, positive or constructive the popular saying: „Man learns from mistakes". Man, on the contrary should learn only from his successes and from those who have achieved successes and gained, by imitating those positive behaviors, which have effectively contributed to success. In addition man can learn enormously not to have failures, or make mistakes from the knowledge and positive experience of mankind stored in books, media, on the Internet and the experience of people who have huge experience and knowledge. The more we can prevent more failures, mistakes, the more we can prevent more and more different negative effects. It would be necessary and useful the development of a science to prevent human errors because it would prevent a large number of human errors and failures if people study and apply it as much and in as many actions as they can. This knowledge could and should be studied in colleges and universities and other educational forms. In every area of activity for each action type, it could identify factors that create human mistakes and failures and then it could identify solutions and measures to be taken to prevent mistakes and failures. Efforts and expenses that will be done by creating, developing, learning and applicating the science to prevent human errors will not be much lower than the positive effects of their prevention of a very large number of mistakes and failures and their multiple, diverse and very large negative effects. Financial investment, energy, time, etc.. in these activities related to the prevention of human errors and failures would be very effective and necessary and useful for both countries and for people in particular. Each of us in a greater or lesser way can participate in the creation, development and application of the science to prevent human errors.

322. It is essential that much more women set as goals the prevention of divorce, of unhappy marriages and that they work to achieve them, because fortunately they will most certainly succeed because many have the qualities and capabilities required to do this.

Capacities

323. Our necessary capacities including those necessary to the achievement of personal objectives can be formed, developed, maintained and used through the contribution of the formation, development, maintenance and usage of the ability to efficiently organize.

324. Those who control circumstances have greater capacities to participate in achieving the greater good.

325. Those who willingly expand their positive experience have greater capacities to efficiently co-develop.

326. Those who control circumstances have more capacities of achieving more and greater successes.

327. Creative attitudes, qualities and capacities must be rewarded.

328. As we have more capacities and qualities, the more chances we have to meet several favorable occasions.

329. Ideas come fast and we forget them even faster. Ideas come out continuously, without us making any effort. Ideas that we seek, that we want to find we sometimes find them easily, other times very difficult and sometimes we can not fiind anything without looking   better.
Our ability to create ideas is a mine which can increase the value and on a continuous basis,   without   great   efforts.
Our ability to create ideas can continuously

increase for as long as we live, thus increasing its value on a continuous basis. Our ability to create ideas affects us enormously in our achievement and maintenance of our happiness every day in every situation.

One of the objectives of each personal man is necessary and should be the continuous development as much as the ability to create useful, efficient, positive, humane ideas, which can contribute to the achievement of our personal happiness and maintain it. As we grow with a grater ability to create positive, effective ideas, necessary to us, the more and more surely we can achieve personal goals and happiness and we can maintain them.

The ability to produce positive effective ideas, necessary to us is enormously useful and effective as it helps establish, develop, maintain other capacities as well which we can exemplify: 1) the ability to prevent mistakes and failures, 2) the ability to solve problems, 3) our ability to create and maintain happiness; 4) our ability to create, select, set and achieve personal goals; 5) our professional ability, 6) the ability to face any blows of life as big and as painful as they would be; 7) the ability to create and maintain a family, a happy marriage. The ability to produce positive effective ideas can increase greatly, easily and with minimum expenditure, with the help of the Internet, knowledge, positive models, which we can find using the Internet. Until the creation and development of science and broadcasting them in an easy way for each, which includes the ability to create positive effective ideas, necessary to us, respectively the creation of science, the creativity of each of us, it is necessary to look in the edited books, in the media and on the Internet, whenever existing knowledge is needed.

Charming

330. Communication helps us become charming.

331. Our own happiness can be achieved and maintained also through the contribution of the formation, development, maintenance and usage of charming behavior.

332. We can prevent the falling apart of a happy marriage also through the contribution of the

formation, development, maintenance and usage of charming behavior.

333. The necessary qualities in achieving personal goals can be formed, developed, maintained and used also through the contribution of the formation, development, maintenance and usage of charming behavior.

334. Our happiness depends a lot also on the formation, development, maintenance and usage of charming behavior.

335. Rather than lamenting that we do not have successes it is more useful to also form, develop, maintain and use charming behavior.

336. In order to rise up once again for the first time for the who knows what time it is necessary to also form, develop, maintain and use charming behavior.

337. The force of our ideas can be augmented also through the contribution of the formation, development, maintenance and usage of charming behavior.

338. Stress can be prevented also through the formation, development, maintenance and usage of charming behavior.

339. Continuous self-motivation helps us become charming.

340. Pessimism can be removed and replaced with optimism also through the contribution of the formation, development, maintenance and usage of charming behavior.

341. We can become stronger and we can not allow ourselves to be influenced by the world also through the contribution of the formation, development, maintenance and usage of charming behavior.

342. The solutions to the problems we have or that we want to solve can be found also through the contribution of the formation, development, maintenance and usage of charming behavior.

343. Creativity helps us become charming.

344. We can overcome the difficulties that we must overcome also through the help of the formation, development, maintenance and usage of charming behavior.

345. Wisdom helps us become charming.

346. In order to escape poverty it is necessary to also form, develop, maintain and use charming behavior.

347. We can prevent some failures also through the contribution of the formation, development, maintenance and usage of charming behavior.

348. Responsibility helps us become charming.

349. The self efficient use of our time helps us become charming.

Communication

350. Communication helps us become charming.

351. Communication helps us become initiating.

352. Communication helps us become diplomatic.

353. Communication helps us become energetic.

354. Communication helps us become daring.

355. Communication helps us become rulers.

356. Communication helps us become bold.

357. Communication helps us become strong.

358. Communication helps us become decent.

359. Communication helps us become constant.

360. Communication helps us become meticulous.

361. Communication helps us become stimulating.

362. Communication helps us become expansive.

363. Communication helps us become funny.

364. Communication helps us become loyal.

365. Communication helps us become respectful.

366. Communication helps us become confident.

367. Communication helps us become harmless.

368. Communication helps us become independent.

369. Communication helps us become sociable.

370. Communication helps us become liked.

371. Communication helps us become rigorous.

372. Communication helps us become flexible.

373. Communication helps us become decisive.

374. Communication helps us become cheerful.

375. Communication helps us become spiritual.

376. Communication helps us become profound.

377. Communication helps us become mannered.

378. Communication helps us become analytic.

379. Communication helps us become cultivated.

380. Communication helps us become popular.

381. Communication helps us become trained.

382. Communication helps us become selfless.

383. Communication helps us become convincing.

384. Communication helps us become self controlled.

385. Communication helps us become adaptable.

386. Communication helps us become animated.

387. Communication helps us become capable.

388. Communication helps us become sincere.

389. Communication helps us become positive.

390. Communication helps us become leaders.

391. Communication helps us become agreeable.

392. Communication helps us become attachable.

393. Communication helps us become good listeners.

394. Communication helps us become active.

Concentration

395. Permanent concentration on our personal objectives helps us achieve more efficient co operations.

396. Permanent concentration on our personal objectives helps us achieve more favorable situations.

397. Total concentration on personal goals helps us achieve more true friendships.

398. Permanent concentration on our personal objectives helps us achieve more pleasant surprises.

399. Total concentration on personal goals helps us achieve more performances.

400. Permanent concentration on our personal objectives helps us achieve more favorable chances.

401. Permanent concentration on our personal objectives helps us achieve more successes.

402. Total concentration on personal goals helps us achieve more pleasant surprises.

403. Permanent concentration on our personal objectives helps us achieve more personal goals.

404. Total concentration on personal goals helps us achieve more efficient co operations.

405. Total concentration on personal goals helps us achieve much good luck.

406. Permanent concentration on our personal objectives helps us achieve more performances.

407. Total concentration on personal goals helps us achieve more favorable situations.

408. Permanent concentration on our personal objectives helps us achieve much good luck.

409. Total concentration on personal goals helps us achieve more personal goals.

410. Permanent concentration on our personal objectives helps us achieve more true friendships.

411. Permanent concentration on our personal objectives helps us achieve more records.

412. Total concentration on personal goals helps us achieve more favorable chances.

413.   The increased capacity of concentration of our attention helps us and contributes to increasing our efficiency in what we do.

414.   To achieve quality actions to become happy and maintain our happiness, it is necessary that every time we act to focus totally on that action, to be careful in everything we do. Any little distraction can have grater or smaller negative effects on our happiness. Because of this, our happiness totally depends on our overall happiness and on the quality of actions which we achieve, on the concentration and attention with which we perform them.

Confidence

415.   Confidence in the idea that we can create our luck helps us achieve more efficient co operations.

416.   Confidence in the idea that we can create our luck helps us achieve more performances.

417.   Confidence in the success of what we do helps us achieve more records.

418.   Confidence in the success of what we do helps us achieve more efficient co operations.

419. Self confidence helps us achieve more successes.

420. Confidence in the idea that we can create our luck helps us achieve more favorable situations.

421. Confidence in the success of what we do helps us achieve more favorable chances.

422. Self confidence helps us achieve more performances.

423. Self confidence helps us achieve more true friendships.

424. Self confidence helps us achieve more pleasant surprises.

425. Confidence in the success of what we do helps us achieve more true friendships.

426. Self confidence helps us achieve more efficient co operations.

427. Confidence in the idea that we can create our luck helps us achieve more favorable chances.

428. Self confidence helps us achieve more favorable situations.

429. Self confidence helps us achieve much good luck.

430. Confidence in the success of what we do helps us achieve more successes.

431. Self confidence helps us achieve more favorable chances.

432. Confidence in the success of what we do helps us achieve much good luck.

433. Self confidence helps us achieve more records.

434. Confidence in the idea that we can create our luck helps us achieve more successes.

435. Confidence in the success of what we do helps us achieve more pleasant surprises.

436. Confidence in the idea that we can create our luck helps us achieve more records.

437. Confidence in the idea that we can create our luck helps us achieve more true friendships.

438. Confidence in the idea that we can create our luck helps us achieve more personal goals.

439. Confidence in the idea that we can create our luck helps us achieve much good luck.

440. Confidence in the success of what we do helps us achieve more favorable situations.

441. Confidence in the success of what we do helps us achieve more performances.

442. Confidence in the idea that we can create our luck helps us achieve more pleasant surprises.

443. Self confidence helps us achieve more personal goals.

444. A great capacity of increasing self confidence must be imitated.

445. A great capacity of maintaining self confidence helps us maintain our way of being loved.

446. Confidence in ourselves must be appreciated.

447. A great capacity of increasing self confidence helps us become enthusiastic.

448. A great capacity of increasing self confidence helps us become tolerant.

449. Confidence in ourselves helps us become understanding.

450. Confidence in ourselves helps us achieve much more pleasant surprises.

451. A great capacity of maintaining self confidence helps us become more productive.

452. A great capacity of maintaining self confidence helps us become understanding.

453. Confidence in ourselves helps us become energetic.

454. A great capacity of maintaining self confidence must be maintained.

455. A great capacity of maintaining self confidence helps us become more cautious.

Conflicts

456. Finding creative solutions that contribute to solving conflicts helps us achieve more records.

457. Preventing conflicts helps us achieve more personal goals.

458. Preventing conflicts helps us achieve more favorable chances.

459. The ability to solve conflicts helps us achieve more successes.

460. Preventing conflicts helps us achieve more successes.

461. Finding creative solutions that contribute to solving conflicts helps us achieve more favorable chances.

462. Finding creative solutions that contribute to solving conflicts helps us achieve more favorable situations.

463. Finding creative solutions that contribute to solving conflicts helps us achieve much good luck.

464. The ability to solve conflicts helps us achieve more favorable situations.

465. The art of solving conflicts helps us achieve more performances.

466. The ability to solve conflicts helps us achieve more pleasant surprises.

467. Preventing conflicts helps us achieve more true friendships.

468. Finding creative solutions that contribute to solving conflicts helps us achieve more successes.

469. The art of solving conflicts helps us achieve more true friendships.

470. The ability to solve conflicts helps us achieve much good luck.

471. The ability to solve conflicts helps us achieve more records.

472. The art of solving conflicts helps us achieve more records.

473. The ability to solve conflicts helps us achieve more efficient co operations.

474. Preventing conflicts helps us achieve much good luck.

475. Finding creative solutions that contribute to solving conflicts helps us achieve more efficient co operations.

476. The art of solving conflicts helps us achieve more successes.

477. The art of solving conflicts helps us achieve more personal goals.

478. The art of solving conflicts helps us achieve more pleasant surprises.

479. Finding creative solutions that contribute to solving conflicts helps us achieve more personal goals.

480. The art of solving conflicts helps us achieve more efficient co operations.

481. The ability to solve conflicts helps us achieve more true friendships.

482. Preventing conflicts helps us achieve more favorable situations.

483. Preventing conflicts helps us achieve more records.

484. Preventing conflicts helps us achieve more performances.

485. The art of solving conflicts helps us achieve more favorable chances.

486. Finding creative solutions that contribute to solving conflicts helps us achieve more performances.

487. Preventing conflicts helps us achieve more efficient co operations.

488. The ability to solve conflicts helps us achieve more performances.

489. The art of solving conflicts helps us achieve much good luck.

490. The ability to solve conflicts helps us achieve more personal goals.

491. Finding creative solutions that contribute to solving conflicts helps us achieve more true friendships.

492. The art of solving conflicts helps us achieve more favorable situations.

493. The ability to solve conflicts helps us achieve more favorable chances.

494. Finding creative solutions that contribute to solving conflicts helps us achieve more pleasant surprises.

495. Life is much more beautiful in a marriage when there are no conflicts between spouses.

496. By developing their inner beauty, women also develop their abilities that can help them prevent certain conflicts.

497. The self-control of our behaviors helps us a lot to prevent some conflicts.

498. A vigilant man has more chances to prevent more conflicts.

Correct

499. Our chances of becoming happy increase if we establish our personal goals correctly.

500. Our chances of becoming happy increase if we plan our actions correctly.

501. Our chances of becoming happy increase if we are correctly organize.

502. Successes in life can also be achieved thanks to the correct establishment of our personal goals.

503. Our way of seeing family relations, if it is correct helps us a lot to achieve a happy marriage.

504. Our way of seeing family relations can be correct or incorrect.

505. Our way of seeing love relations, if it is incorrect stops the achievement of true love.

506. Our way of seeing love relations, if it is correct helps us a lot to achieve a true love.

507. Our way of seeing love relations can be correct or incorrect.

508. Correct appreciations are appreciated a lot.

509. He who makes correct appreciations is esteemed by people.

510. He who makes correct appreciations is appreciated a lot by people.

511. People want to be appreciated correctly.

512. Illegal accusations can be prevented by effective laws and their correct application.

513. Mutual correct appreciations maintain friendships.

514. Those who see life in an incorrect way have a lot to suffer in life.

515. When we see life in an incorrect way it harms us a lot.

516. Developing our thinking can be achieved also through the formation, development,

maintenance and usage of a correct life conception.

517. We can become stronger and we cannot let ourselves be influenced by the world also through the contribution of the formation, development, maintenance and usage of a correct life conception.

518. Correct thinking can be formed, developed and used also through the contribution of the formation, development, maintenance and usage of all only objective ideas.

519. Forming vices can be prevented also through the contribution of the formation, development, maintenance and usage of correct behaviors.

520. We can replace wrong ideas with correct ideas also through the contribution of the formation, development, maintenance and usage of efficient ideas.

521. Stress can be prevented also through the contribution of the formation, development, maintenance and usage of correct behaviors.

522. Emancipation from restrictions can be achieved if we use our time correctly.

523. We can make correct decisions if we know ourselves.

524. In order not to let ourselves be overwhelmed by the difficulties of life it is necessary to form, develop, maintain and use a correct life conception.

525. Forming wrong ideas can be prevented through the contribution of the formation, development, maintenance and usage of correct thinking.

526. Emancipation from restrictions can be made through the formation, development, maintenance and usage of correct thinking.

527. We can prevent the falling apart of a happy marriage also through the contribution of the formation, development, maintenance and usage of correct behaviors.

528. Pessimism can be removed through the contribution of the formation, development, maintenance and usage of correct thinking.

529. A correct thinking can be formed by using logical thinking.

530. We can replace wrong ideas with correct ideas through finding and using correct ideas.

531. The meaning of life can be found through the contribution of the formation, development, maintenance and usage of correct ideas.

Character

532. Sometimes luck appears only because we have a character.

533. People who have had successes are people of character.

534. A responsible man is also a man of character.

535. A man's character can create many riches, but riches can not give back the character if it is lost.

536. Those who have as a personal objective the harmonious development of their character will succeed in life and achieve a more beautiful life than those who do not have among their personal goals the harmonious development of their personality.

537. Those who have as a personal objective the harmonious development of their character will succeed in life to achieve more successes and far fewer failures than those who do not have personal objectives and do not target their own harmonious development of their personality.

538. The man who has no good sense has no character.

539. Moral wealth is given by the moral character and values that each of us has.

Credibility

540. Moral values continuously increase our credibility.

541. Solving problems through positive methods increases our credibility.

542. Those who discover unique ways to work efficiently for a better life increase their credibility.

543. A positive conception of life increases our credibility.

544. Long term thinking increases our credibility.

545. Constructive thinking increases our credibility.

546. Those who control circumstances increase their credibility.

547. Those who willingly expand their positive experience increase their credibility.

548. Efficient people in positive actions have more chances of increasing their credibility.

549. Those who know that discipline is one of the keys of dreams increased their credibility.

550. The sense of objectivity increases the credibility of the person who has it.

551. Sometimes the lack of common sense enormously reduces the credibility of the ones who do not have common sense.

552. Concentrating our energies increases our credibility.

553. A non hostile but aggressive behavior helps us increase our credibility.

554. People who are resistant to stress have a greater credibility.

555. Credibility many times brings us luck.

556. A positive enterprising spirit increases our credibility.

557. The sense of credibility helps us become more credible.

558. The sense of fairness increases our credibility.

559. Those who know how to take advantage of the opportunity to create increase their credibility.

560. Solving problems only through constructive methods increases our credibility.

Creative

561.   Creative people are always young spirituals.

562.   People who are always concerned about the future also have creative qualities.

563.   Creative people have a futurological thought on a long term.

564.   Creative people have a great capacity to create projects.

565.   People can develop their creative potential for as long as they live.

566.   The more creative qualities we have and the greater capacity of creation, the more we can find and discover more favorable circumstances for ourselves.

567.   Creative ideas help us get performance.

568.   It is necessary that we all contribute to forge a creative society.

569.   The creative society makes everyone happier.

570.   Creative people should be helped to create as much as possible.

571. The creative attitudes that we do not have we must form to help us become more creative.

572. The more creative we are, the greater capacity of creation we have, the more opportunities we have to meet several favorable occasions.

573. In life for as long as we live, it is necessary and useful to develop continuously, day by day, our creative skills and our creative abilities.

574. Our personal objective of the self-development of our creative skills, day by day, helps and contributes greatly to achieving our other personal objectives.

575. For as long as we live, continuously, day by day, it is necessary to have as a personal goal to form and develop as more creative qualities as we can.

576. How we live day by day, achieving the target of personal training and development of our creative skills helps and contributes greatly to achieving other personal objectives.

577. The more creative qualities we shape and develop, the more creative we become.

578. The orientation towards everything new is a creative attitude that helps us a lot to achieve personal goals.

579. If a person does not have creative attitude, a shift towards everything new, he can shape and develop it.

580. Confidence in our own forces is a creative attitude that helps us and contributes greatly to achieve our personal goals.

581. A person who has no creative attitude, confidence in his own forces, he can auto-shape it, develop and maintain it for life.

582. The diversity of interests is a creative attitude that helps us a lot to achieve personal goals.

583. A person who has no creative attitude, diversity of interests can auto-shape, develop and maintain it for as long as he lives.

584. Our orientation towards a very distant future is a creative attitude that helps us a lot to achieve our personal goals.

585. The ability to use the completion of ideas is a creative attitude that helps us a lot to achieve our personal goals.

586. A person who does not have the attitude of complete creative ideas in the state that it can be useful, can also auto shape it, develop and maintain it for as long as he lives. Good luck.

587. The diversity of our interests is a creative attitude that helps us a lot to be more creative.

588. The diversity of our interests is a creative attitude that helps us a lot more to resolve problems more quickly.

589. A person who has no creative attitude oriented towards the future can auto-shape, develop and maintain it for as long as he lives. Good luck.

590. The creative attitude oriented towards the future helps us very much to resolve more problems more quickly.

591. The ability to mobilize is a creative attitude that helps us become more creative.

592. We can create a beautiful life for ourselves if we have creative attitudes.

593. Each of us needs to pay attention to the development required for a creative thinking.

594. Expectations are creative roads for us.

595. Young people are more receptive to creative ideas.

596. In life we have more opportunities to meet favorable situations if we are friends with as many people who have had successes as possible, people which have qualities, skills, effective behaviors, creative qualities, which are well documented in the areas that concern us as well.

597. Creative thinking helps us very much to achieve performances.

598. Negative thinking is the creative of many human misfortunes.

599. Only positive thinking can create positive creative ideas.

600. The formation and development of the creative thinking of every person by the state

is a necessity and an obligation of each state.

601. Thinking creatively contributes greatly to the achievement of personal goals.

602. Creative thinking helps us have more opportunities to meet more favorable situations in life.

603. Creative thinking will help us greatly increase the efficiency of the use of our time.

604. Hopes are the creatives of joy.

605. Psychological discomfort greatly decreases the effectiveness of creative abilities.

606. The psychological comfort of the family helps us create the opportunity to become more creative and more effective in creativity.

607. Creative behavior helps us achieve much faster our personal goals.

608. Creative behavior helps us achieve more effective co operations.

609. Creative behavior helps us have many more opportunities to meet more favorable circumstances.

610. Creative behavior helps us very much to become more efficient much faster.

611. We can make our life more beautiful and if we have creative attitudes.

612. Each of us is necessary to pay the attention necessary to developing our creative thinking.

613. In life we have many more chances to meet favorable situations if we are friends with as many people as we can who have had successes, who have qualities, skills, effective behaviors, creative qualities, which are well documented in areas that concern us all.

614. Creative thinking helps us very much to obtain performances.

615. Increasing our ability to concentrate makes us more creative.

616. Harmonious global co-development thinking leads to use long term thinking, creative thinking, humanist thinking, social thinking, etc.

617. Creative thinking contributes a lot to forming, developing and promoting harmonious global co-development thinking.

618. Although forming and developing a creative thinking helps us achieve our personal objectives many of us do not use it.

619. Each of us must give the attention and time needed to form and develop continuously our creative thinking.

620. Creative thinking helps us solve problems that apparently are impossible to solve.

621. Creative thinking helps us a lot to find the right partners for efficient co operations.

622. Creative thinking can help us a lot to prevent stress and recover after stress.

623. Creative ideas help us achieve personal goals.

624. Creative ideas help us have more chances to meet favorable situations.

625. Creative ideas help us achieve a pleasant and happy life.

626. By continuously developing our creative ideas we will become more efficient.

627. The larger our creative capacity is the more chances we have of achieving our objectives.

628. Creative attitudes, qualities and capacities must be rewarded.

629. Those willing to try new ways are creative.

630. A man willing to try new ways has many creative qualities.

631. Methods of creation help us increase our creative capacity.

632. The more knowledge we have and the more creative methods we apply the more chances we have to achieve personal goals.

633. Creative ideas help us a lot to increase our chances to meet more favorable situations.

634. Creative ideas help us a lot to increase our chances to achieve personal goals.

635. Constructive thinking helps us become more creative.

636. Each of us can be free in thought only due to preconceptions, superstitions and the absence of the necessary knowledge and of creative attitudes.

637. Creative attitudes contribute a lot in spiritual self development.

638. Creative attitudes contribute a lot and mental self development.

639. Most of those involved in several projects also have creative qualities.

640. Those who are remarkably gifted can become more creative a lot faster.

641. Those who are remarkably gifted many times have a creative thinking.

642. A positive enterprising spirit makes each of us more creative.

643. Those who are oriented towards lasting success are mostly creative.

644. The need to succeed makes people more creative.

645. A creative man has many chances and high possibilities of having luck.

646. A creative man has a greater potential to become more efficient.

647. Those who live life fully and not at random are usually more creative in most occasions.

648. Those who have the opportunities to develop have greater chances to become more creative.

649. Efficient people in positive actions are also creative.

650. People with human social behaviors need to have a creative thinking.

651. A man open towards new ideas has much more chances and a much greater potential to become more creative.

652. Creative people are engines of progress in all areas of activity.

653. The creative man has much more chances and a higher potential to achieve more and greater successes.

654. Curious people are more creative.

655. A creative man must be appreciated, promoted, supported and rewarded.

656. A creative man has many chances and a greater potential to achieve more and greater performances.

657. People who have the ability to support ideas are very creative.

658. He who is oriented towards routine has small chances of being creative.

659. People with wrong ideas because of some wrong ideas cannot be creative.

660. We can broaden our horizon even more through the contribution of the formation, development, maintenance and usage of a positive conception of creative life.

661. The release from the restrictions imposed by ourselves can be made also through the contribution of the formation, development, maintenance and usage of a creative thinking.

662. Those who solve problems only through constructive methods are also creative.

663. Long term thinking makes us become more creative.

664. Those who have no hopes, in order to create their hopes in the future need to form and developed their creative thinking.

665. Those who have no hopes, in order to create their hopes in the future they need to connect with people who are creative.

666. Most of those who wander without a purpose in life are less creative.

667. People who know how to take quality decisions also have a creative thinking.

668. Those who have high objectives in life are mostly creative.

669. The sense of quality makes us also be creative.

670. The sense of achieving quality in everything we do makes us become creative even if we are not creative.

671. Those who do not have hopes, in order to create hopes for the future, need to connect with people who also have a creative thinking.

672. Those who discover unique ways to work efficiently for a better life are creative people.

673. Those who have high objectives in life mostly have a creative thinking.

674. People who have the ability to take rapid quality decisions have many creative qualities.

675. Those who willingly expand their positive experience are also creative.

676. The desire to make others happy can be really achieved through the contribution of the formation, development, maintenance and usage of creative ideas.

677. Forming wrong ideas can be prevented also through the formation, development, maintenance and usage of creative thinking.

678. Preventing the formation of doubts can be achieved also through the formation, development, maintenance and usage of creative thinking.

679. Hopes can be created also through the contribution of the formation, development, maintenance and usage of a creative life conception.

680. We can overcome difficulties that we must overcome also through the formation, development and maintenance of creative thinking.

681. In order to change the desire of changing into reality it is necessary to form, develop, maintain and use creative thinking.

682. Preventing the formation of doubts can also be achieved through the formation, development, maintenance and usage of a creative life conception.

683. Finding the meaning of our lives can be achieved also through the contribution of the formation, development, maintenance and usage of a creative life conception.

684. We can prevent some failures also through the contribution of the formation, development, maintenance and usage of creative behaviors.

685. Hopes can be created also through the contribution of formation, development, maintenance and usage of creative ideas.

Creativity

686. The capacity of stimulating creativity in others helps us a lot in maintaining efficient co operations.

687. The ability of stimulating creativity in others helps us a lot to achieve our personal goals.

688. The ability to stimulate creativity in others helps us a lot to achieve more and greater successes.

689. Pessimism can be removed through the contribution of the formation, development, maintenance and usage of creativity.

690. Ignorance can be avoided through creativity and study.

691. Hopes can be created through creativity.

692. Personal goals can be achieved through creativity.

693. We can form, develop, maintain and use an open mind by using creativity.

694. Creativity assures a better life for us.

695. The development of creativity increases our chances of achieving our personal objectives.

696. The ability to stimulate other people's creativity is rewarded with successes.

697. The creative man develops his creativity more and more.

698. Creativity must be encouraged.

699. Creativity must be appreciated.

700. Creativity must be rewarded.

701. Creativity must be supported.

702. Creativity can be formed.

703. Creativity can be developed.

704. Creativity can be enhanced.

705. Creativity helps us achieve more true friendships.

706. Creativity helps us achieve a true love.

707. Creativity helps us become perfectionists.

708. Creativity helps us become audacious.

709. A great capacity of increasing creativity helps us become tolerant.

710. A great capacity of increasing creativity helps us maintain our way of being practical.

711. Creativity helps us become self controlled.

712. A great capacity of increasing creativity helps us become optimistic.

713. Creativity helps us become rigorous.

714. Creativity helps us become animated.

715. A great capacity of increasing creativity helps us become happy.

716. Creativity helps us become energetic.

717. A great capacity of increasing creativity helps us become understanding.

718. A great capacity of increasing creativity helps us maintain our way of being loving.

719. Creativity helps us become cheerful.

720. A great capacity of increasing creativity must be encouraged.

721. A great capacity of increasing creativity helps us become wise.

722. Creativity helps us become spontaneous.

723. A great capacity of increasing creativity helps us achieve more personal goals.

724. A great capacity of increasing creativity helps us become more productive.

725. Creativity helps us become spiritual.

726. Creativity helps us become persevering.

727. Creativity helps us become analytic.

728. Creativity helps us become leaders.

729. Creativity helps us become voluble.

730. A great capacity of increasing creativity helps us maintain our way of being cautious.

731. A great capacity of increasing creativity helps us become more humane.

732. Creativity helps us become rulers.

733. A great capacity of increasing creativity helps us become more preventive.

734. Creativity helps us become respectful.

735. Creativity helps us become sturdy.

736. Creativity helps us become mannered.

737. Creativity helps us become cultivated.

738. A great capacity of increasing creativity helps us become loving.

739. Creativity helps us become good listeners.

740. A great capacity of increasing creativity must be appreciated.

741. Creativity helps us become penetrating.

742. Creativity helps us become joyful.

743. Creativity helps us become peacemakers.

744. Creativity helps us become convincing.

745. Creativity helps us become reserved.

746. A great capacity of increasing creativity helps us become more cautious.

747. A great capacity of increasing creativity helps us become happier.

748. A great capacity of increasing creativity helps us become more optimistic.

749. Creativity helps us become pleasant.

750. A great capacity of increasing creativity helps us maintain our happiness.

751. A great capacity of increasing creativity must be developed.

752. A great capacity of increasing creativity helps us become more tolerant.

753. A great capacity of increasing creativity helps us achieve more efficient co operations.

754. Creativity helps us become strong.

755. A great capacity of increasing creativity helps us maintain our way of being liked.

756. A great capacity of increasing creativity helps us become loved.

757. Creativity helps us become adaptable.

758. A great capacity of increasing creativity helps us maintain our wisdom.

759. Creativity helps us become confident.

760. A great capacity of increasing creativity helps us become efficient.

761. A great capacity of increasing creativity must be supported.

762. Creativity helps us become sensitive.

763. A great capacity of increasing creativity helps us become practical.

764. A great capacity of increasing creativity must be imitated.

765. A great capacity of increasing creativity helps us become more pleasant.

766. Creativity helps us become peaceful.

767. Creativity helps us become harmless.

768. Creativity helps us become active.

769. Creativity helps us become organized.

770. A great capacity of increasing creativity helps us achieve more successes.

771. A great capacity of increasing creativity helps us become more practical.

772. Creativity helps us become independent.

773. Creativity helps us become content.

774. Creativity helps us become diplomatic.

775. A great capacity of increasing creativity helps us become more loving.

776. Creativity helps us become unpretentious.

777. A great capacity of increasing creativity must be a model.

778. Creativity helps us become attachable.

779. Creativity helps us become tenacious.

780. Creativity helps us become fighting.

781. A great capacity of increasing creativity helps us achieve more true friendships.

782. Creativity helps us become balanced.

783. A great capacity of increasing creativity must be used.

784. A great capacity of increasing creativity helps us become more enthusiastic.

Circumstances

785. Those who control circumstances have greater chances of becoming more efficient.

786. Those who control circumstances must be promoted.

787. Those who control circumstances have a greater potential to succeed.

788. People who have success have controlled circumstances many times.

789. Those who control circumstances can control them better if they make necessary exchanges of information.

790. Those who control circumstances have greater capacities to participate in achieving the greater good.

791. Those who control circumstances continuously develop their trust in the future.

792. Those who control circumstances have a greater ability to maintain true friendships.

793. Those who control circumstances have a greater potential to maintain a happy marriage.

794. Those who control circumstances have a high capacity to achieve personal goals.

795. Those who control circumstances have more chances to find the right partner for life.

796. Those who control circumstances have more capacities of achieving more and greater successes.

797. Those who control circumstances are engines of progress in all areas of activities.

798. The world must legislate the obligation of putting recordings on the Internet of court sentences, of all documents related to the process, files, everything that is public information, except the circumstances stipulated by law when sentences are not public.

799. The Internet helps us have more chances to meet much more favorable circumstances.

800. Some successes are due mostly to favorable circumstances and a lot less to people.

801. Spiritual self-development done continuously, day by day, for as long as we live greatly increases our chances to have more opportunities to meet much more favorable circumstances.

802. Effective co operations increase our chances to meet more favorable circumstances.

803. Calculated people are more likely to encounter much more favorable circumstances.

804. Those who have more skills have more opportunities to encounter much more favorable circumstances.

805. Creative behavior helps us have many more opportunities to meet more favorable circumstances.

806. Cooperative behavior helps us have more opportunities to meet more favorable circumstances.

807. The more experienced we are in a particular area the better chances we have to meet more favorable circumstances.

Daring

808. Optimism helps us become daring.

809. We can contribute to the achievement of our greatest accomplishments also through the contribution of the formation, development, maintenance and usage of daring behavior.

810. Positive experience can be achieved also through the contribution of the formation, development, maintenance and usage of daring behavior.

811. Release from our self-imposed restrictions can be made also through the contribution of the formation, development, maintenance and usage of daring behavior.

812. Confidence in ourselves helps us become daring.

813. In order to rise up once again for the first time for the who knows what time it is necessary to also form, develop, maintain and use daring behavior.

814.   Acting efficiently helps us become daring.

815.   The radical transformation for the better of our life can be achieved also through the formation, development, maintenance and usage of daring behavior.

816.   Self-imposed discipline helps us become daring.

817.   In order to prevent failures it is necessary to also form, develop, maintain and use daring behavior.

818.   The force of our ideas can be augmented also through the contribution of the formation, development, maintenance and usage of daring behavior.

819.   Continuously making ourselves efficient helps us become daring.

820.   We can overcome the difficulties that we must overcome also through the help of the formation, development, maintenance and usage of daring behavior.

821.   Stress can be prevented also through the formation, development, maintenance and usage of daring behavior.

822. Responsibility helps us become daring.

823. Continuous self-motivation helps us become daring.

824. Obtaining more and greater successes can be achieved also through the contribution of the formation, development, maintenance, usage of a daring behavior.

825. Our future can be projected and achieved also through the contribution of the formation, development, maintenance and usage of daring behavior.

826. We can prevent the falling apart of a happy marriage also through the contribution of the formation, development, maintenance and usage of daring behavior.

Decisions

827. In order to trace and transform our personal objectives into reality it is necessary to form, develop, maintain and use the ability to take rapid quality decisions.

828. Obtaining more and greater successes can be achieved also through the contribution of the formation, development, maintenance

and usage of a greater capacity to take rapid quality decisions.

829. In order to take correct decisions it is necessary to form, develop, maintain and use the ability to be responsible.

830. The ability to take rapid decisions increases our possibilities to prevent many unpleasant surprises.

831. The ability to take rapid decisions increases our chances to achieve efficient co-developments.

832. Young people need and must implicate themselves in taking all the decisions that affect them directly or indirectly.

833. The ability to take rapid decisions increases our capacity of achieving outstanding performances.

834. The ability to take rapid decisions increases our possibilities of achieving our personal goals a lot faster.

835. Most people who have had successes know how to take rapid decisions.

836. The ability of taking the rapid decisions increases our efficiency a lot.

837. Our ability of taking rapid decisions helps us have more chances to meet favorable situations.

838. Hesitating behavior reduces the operability of the decisions that we take.

839. All of those who know how to prevent possible mistakes have a greater ability of taking quality decisions.

840. People who know how to take quality decisions develop their sense of industriousness.

841. People who know how to take quality decisions have and develop their sense of self-imposed discipline.

842. People who know how to take quality decisions have a great capacity of maintaining efficient co-developments.

843. People who know how to take quality decisions trust themselves.

844. People who know how to take quality decisions also achieve positive actions.

845. People who know how to take quality decisions have a greater capacity of maintaining a mature love.

846. People who know how to take quality decisions have a greater ability of achieving the positive social relations that they desire.

847. People who have the ability to take rapid quality decisions have a greater capacity to achieve efficient co operations in order to reach their personal goals.

848. People who have the ability of taking rapid quality decisions have more and greater chances to achieve their own happiness.

849. People who have the ability to take rapid decisions have good conditions of achieving the greater good.

850. People who have the ability to take rapid quality decisions also have an anticipative thinking.

851. Those who have objectives in life mostly take efficient decisions.

852. The majority of people who take positive decisions more easily maintain the positive social relations that they have.

853. People who take positive decisions have greater and more chances to achieve themselves.

854. People who take positive decisions mostly have few mistakes and even zero mistakes.

855. People who take positive decisions are mostly credible.

856. People who take positive decisions have more and greater chances to achieve their desired future.

857. People who take positive decisions are engines of development.

858. People who know how to take positive decisions can perfect themselves.

859. Those who know how to take positive decisions have more and greater successes.

860. The majority of decisions have both positive effects as well as negative effects.

861. Wrong decisions must be revealed as being wrong as soon as possible.

862. People who have success have a great capacity of rapidly taking decisions.

Development

863. The obstacles that prevent us from achieving our personal goals can be surpassed also through the contribution of the formation, development, maintenance and usage of spontaneous behavior.

864. We can form, develop and maintain the state of being ourselves also through the contribution of the formation, development, maintenance and usage of a joyful behavior.

865. Positive experience can be achieved also through the contribution of the formation, development, maintenance and usage of a behavior with a theoretic spirit.

866. We can form, develop and maintain the state of being ourselves also through the contribution of the formation, development, maintenance and usage of a cheerful behavior.

867. We can contribute to the achievement of our greatest accomplishments also through the contribution of the formation, development, maintenance and usage of funny behavior.

868. We can overcome the difficulties that we must overcome also through the help of the

formation, development, maintenance and usage of bold behavior.

869.   Our own happiness can be achieved and maintained also through the contribution of the formation, development, maintenance and usage of analytic behavior.

870.   The radical transformation for the better of our life can be achieved also through the formation, development, maintenance and usage of sportive behavior.

871.   Positive experience can be achieved also through the contribution of the formation, development, maintenance and usage of bold behavior.

872.   Our own happiness can be achieved and maintained also through the contribution of the formation, development, maintenance and usage of charming behavior

873.   The radical transformation for the better of our life can be achieved also through the formation, development, maintenance and usage of leading behavior.

874.   Some mistakes can be prevented also through the contribution of the formation,

development, maintenance and usage of imaginative behavior.

875.   We can become stronger and we can not allow ourselves to be influenced by the world also through the contribution of the formation, development, maintenance and usage of sturdy behavior.

876.   Our future can be projected and achieved also through the contribution of the formation, development, maintenance and usage of idealistic behavior.

877.   We can become stronger and we can not allow ourselves to be influenced by the world also through the contribution of the formation, development, maintenance and usage of ingenious behavior.

878.   Our own happiness can be achieved and maintained also through the contribution of the formation, development, maintenance and usage of continuous self perfecting behavior.

879.   Pessimism can be removed and replaced with optimism also through the contribution of the formation, development, maintenance and usage of hardworking behavior.

880. The solutions to the problems we have or that we want to solve can be found also through the contribution of the formation, development, maintenance and usage of respectful behavior.

881. Our own happiness can be achieved and maintained also through the contribution of the formation, development, maintenance and usage of sensible behavior.

882. We can contribute to the achievement of our greatest accomplishments also through the contribution of the formation, development, maintenance and usage of being a good listener behavior.

883. Pessimism can be removed and replaced with optimism also through the contribution of the formation, development, maintenance and usage of a behavior of being devoid of prejudices.

884. The force of our ideas can be augmented also through the contribution of the formation, development, maintenance and usage of sincere behavior.

885. We can prevent the falling apart of a happy marriage also through the contribution of the

formation, development, maintenance and usage of flexible behavior.

886. Our own happiness can be achieved and maintained also through the contribution of the formation, development, maintenance and usage of realistic behavior.

887. The limits of achievement imposed by ourselves in our mind at a given moment can be overcome or eliminated also through the contribution of the formation, development, maintenance and usage of meticulous behavior.

Difficulties

888. We can overcome the difficulties that we must overcome also through the help of the formation, development, maintenance and usage of balanced behavior.

889. We can overcome the difficulties that we must overcome also through the help of the formation, development, maintenance and usage of inventive behavior.

890. We can overcome the difficulties that we must overcome also through the help of the

121

formation, development, maintenance and usage of cheerful behavior.

891. We can overcome the difficulties that we must overcome also through the help of the formation, development, maintenance and usage of initiating behavior.

892. We can overcome the difficulties that we must overcome also through the help of the formation, development, maintenance and usage of agreeable behavior.

893. We can overcome the difficulties that we must overcome also through the help of the formation, development, maintenance and usage of efficient behavior.

894. We can overcome the difficulties that we must overcome also through the help of the formation, development, maintenance and usage of the loyal behavior.

895. We can overcome the difficulties that we must overcome also through the help of the formation, development, maintenance and usage of charming behavior.

896. We can overcome the difficulties that we must overcome also through the help of the

formation, development, maintenance and usage of kind behavior.

897. We can overcome the difficulties that we must overcome also through the help of the formation, development, maintenance and usage of scientific spirit behavior.

898. We can overcome the difficulties that we must overcome also through the help of the formation, development, maintenance and usage of abstract behavior.

899. We can overcome the difficulties that we must overcome also through the help of the formation, development, maintenance and usage of intellectual behavior.

900. We can overcome the difficulties that we must overcome also through the help of the formation, development, maintenance and usage of logical behavior.

901. We can overcome the difficulties that we must overcome also through the help of the formation, development, maintenance and usage of continuous self perfecting behavior.

902. We can overcome the difficulties that we must overcome also through the help of the formation, development, maintenance and usage of positive behavior.

903. We can overcome the difficulties that we must overcome also through the help of the formation, development, maintenance and usage of calm behavior.

904. We can overcome the difficulties that we must overcome also through the help of the formation, development, maintenance and usage of hardworking behavior.

905. We can overcome the difficulties that we must overcome also through the help of the formation, development, maintenance and usage of a behavior of being devoid of prejudices.

906. We can overcome the difficulties that we must overcome also through the help of the formation, development, maintenance and usage of leading behavior.

907. We can overcome the difficulties that we must overcome also through the help of the formation, development, maintenance and usage of analytic behavior.

908. We can overcome the difficulties that we must overcome also through the help of the formation, development, maintenance and usage of animated behavior.

909. We can overcome the difficulties that we must overcome also through the help of the formation, development, maintenance and usage of impersonal behavior.

910. We can overcome the difficulties that we must overcome also through the help of the formation, development, maintenance and usage of adaptable behavior.

911. We can overcome the difficulties that we must overcome also through the help of the formation, development, maintenance and usage of content behavior.

912. We can overcome the difficulties that we must overcome also through the help of the formation, development, maintenance and usage of peacemaking behavior.

913. We can overcome the difficulties that we must overcome also through the help of the formation, development, maintenance and usage of realistic behavior.

914. We can overcome the difficulties that we must overcome also through the help of the formation, development, maintenance and usage of confident behavior.

Discipline

915. Self-imposed discipline helps us become good listeners.

916. Self-imposed discipline helps us become altruistic.

917. Self-imposed discipline helps us become systematic.

918. Self-imposed discipline helps us become confident.

919. Self-imposed discipline helps us become independent.

920. In order to change into reality it is necessary to form, develop, maintain and use the sense of discipline.

921. Problems cannot be solved by the ideas that created them but also through the contribution of the formation, development, maintenance and usage of Self-imposed disciplined behaviors.

922. In order to change the desire of changing into reality it is necessary to form, develop, maintain and use the ability to self-impose the necessary discipline.

923. Forming wrong ideas can be prevented through the contribution of the formation, development, maintenance and usage of the sense of self imposed discipline.

924. The desire to make others happy can be accomplished through the contribution of the formation, development, maintenance and usage of the sense of self imposed discipline.

925. Finding the meaning of life can be achieved through discipline.

926. Our transformation for the better can be achieved through discipline.

927. Discipline can be formed also through the involvement in efficient projects.

928. Discipline can be formed, developed, maintained and used also through the contribution of the formation, development, maintenance and usage of the ability to organize.

929. In order to pursue and transform our personal goals into reality we need to form, develop, maintain and use self-imposed discipline.

930. Discipline can be formed, developed, maintained and used also through the contribution of the formation, development, maintenance and usage of self-imposed discipline.

931. We can overcome the difficulties that we must surpass also through the formation, development, maintenance and usage of the sense of self-imposed discipline.

932. Discipline can be formed, developed, maintained and used also through the contribution of the formation, development, maintenance and usage of the sense of responsibility.

933. In order to pursue and transform our personal goals into reality we need to form, develop, maintain and use the sense of discipline in everything we do.

934. In achieving successes a contribution is brought by the formation, development,

maintenance and usage of behaviors that respect self-imposed discipline.

935. Problems cannot only be solved by the ideas of that created them but also through the contribution of the formation, development, maintenance and usage of behaviors of self-imposed discipline.

936. Problems cannot only be solved by the ideas of that created them but also through the contribution of the formation, development, maintenance and usage of behavior is of self-imposed discipline.

937. In order to change the desire of changing into reality it is necessary to form, develop, maintain and use the ability to impose yourselves with the necessary discipline.

938. Forming wrong ideas can be prevented also through the formation, development, maintenance and usage of self-imposed discipline.

Disappointments

939. Getting out of the state of pessimism can be also achieved by studying theories on disappointments in psychology books.

940. Many of those who have no personal goals have lives that are full of trouble, sufferance, disappointments, failures, etc.

Discourage

941. The self-control of our behaviors helps us a lot to prevent discouragement.

942. Failures in friendships must never discourage us.

943. In order to pursue and transform our personal goals into reality we need to form and develop the ability to be courageous and discouraged.

944. In order to trace and transform our personal goals into reality it is necessary that we form and develop the ability to form courage when we are discouraged.

945. Rather than being discouraged it is a lot better to search for solutions in solving the problems that we have.

946. A failure or failures should not discourage us.

947. Luxury should be discouraged.

948. Failures should never discourage us, because life also offers us many favorable situations to succeed. Through perseverance we will also find those favorable situations that will help us have success.

949. Any injustice that could be done to us should not discourage us.

950. If our objectives seem achievable to us, and many people consider them achievable without proof of evidence, their support should not discourage us.

951. Failures should never discourage us.

Eager

952. Release from our self-imposed restrictions can be made also through the contribution of the formation, development, maintenance and usage of a behavior eager for knowledge.

953. Our happiness depends a lot also on the formation, development, maintenance and usage of a behavior of being eager for knowledge.

954. We can overcome the difficulties that we must overcome also through the help of the formation, development.

955. Acting efficiently helps us become eager for knowledge.

956. Maintenance and usage of a behavior of being eager for knowledge.

957. Problems cannot be solved by the ideas that created them but also through the contribution of the formation, development, maintenance and usage of a behavior of being eager for knowledge.

958. Obtaining more and greater successes can be achieved also through the contribution of the formation, development, maintenance, usage of a behavior eager for knowledge.

959. In order to prevent not achieving our personal goals, it is necessary to also form, develop, maintain and use our behavior of being eager for knowledge.

960. Our resistance to changing for the better can be overcome also through the contribution of the formation, development, maintenance

and usage of a behavior eager for knowledge.

961. Aspiring towards a more meaningful life can also be achieved through the formation, development, maintenance and usage of a behavior of being eager for knowledge.

962. Stress can be prevented also through the formation, development, maintenance and usage of a behavior of being eager for knowledge.

963. Positive experience can be achieved also through the contribution of the formation, development, maintenance and usage of a behavior eager for knowledge.

964. In achieving our successes a contribution is also brought by the formation, development, maintenance and usage of a behavior of being eager for knowledge.

965. In order to rise up once again for the first time for the who knows what time it is necessary to also form, develop, maintain and use a behavior of being eager for knowledge.

966. We can prevent the falling apart of a happy marriage also through the contribution of the formation, development, maintenance and usage of a behavior eager for knowledge.

967. We can prevent some failures also through the contribution of the formation, development, maintenance and usage of a behavior of being eager for knowledge.

968. Our future can be projected and achieved also through the contribution of the formation, development, maintenance and usage of a behavior of being eager for knowledge.

969. We can form, develop and maintain the state of being ourselves also through the contribution of the formation, development, maintenance and usage of a behavior eager for knowledge.

970. We can contribute to the achievement of our greatest accomplishments also through the contribution of the formation, development, maintenance and usage of a behavior eager for knowledge.

Education

971. We can contribute to the achievement of our greatest accomplishments also through the contribution of the formation, development, maintenance and usage of continuous self-education behavior.

972. Successes in life can also be achieved thanks to continuous education.

973. Meanness is also the effect of the absence of our home education.

974. The meaning of life can be found through the contribution of the formation, development, maintenance and usage of self education.

975. Advanced education contributes sensibly to achieving a positive global future.

976. Advanced education contributes extensively to achieving more and greater successes.

977. Advanced education contributes extensively to achieving the future.

978. Educational needs change continuously and they must be satisfied immediately.

979. Humanist education reduces the insecurity of everyday life very much.

980. The education for humanist economy must take the place of the present economical education.

981. Permanent self education used in solving personal problems increases our trust in ourselves and in our possibilities.

982. Permanent self education helps us a lot to achieve more and greater successes.

983. An advanced education contributes greatly to achieving success in life.

984. Self- education for co-development is necessary to be a personal goal for each of us.

Efficiency

985. A great capacity of creating one's own safety helps us maintain our efficiency.

986. A great capacity of being flexible helps us maintain our efficiency.

987. Adaptation helps us maintain efficiency.

988. A great capacity of being as strong as possible helps us maintain our efficiency.

989. A great capacity of learning in order to achieve successes helps us maintain our efficiency.

990. A great capacity of appreciating people helps us maintain our efficiency.

991. A great capacity of learning how to achieve personal goals helps us maintain our efficiency.

992. A great capacity of using abilities helps us maintain our efficiency.

993. The desire to be grand helps us maintain our efficiency.

994. A great capacity of cherishing oneself helps us maintain our efficiency.

995. A great capacity of being tolerant with people helps us maintain our efficiency.

996. A great capacity of being honest with oneself helps us maintain our efficiency.

997. A great capacity of being creative in order to solve great problems helps us maintain our efficiency.

998. The self-control of our behaviors helps us a lot to prevent inefficiency.

999. Those who succeed to more effectively use their personal time must be given a workplace corresponding to their efficiency.

1000. When we work with commitment we have a greater efficiency.

1001. Optimism contributes to achieving a higher efficiency.

1002. Skill increases our efficiency a lot.

1003. We must permanently enhance the efficiency of using creative qualities.

1004. Positive human solidarity increases the efficiency of many human actions a lot.

1005. Forming wrong ideas can be prevented through the contribution of the formation, development, maintenance and usage of the sense of efficiency.

Exceptional

1006. Imagination is a main factor that helps us a lot to deal with exceptional difficult situations.

1007. In 2007 the behaviors of the majority of people in the world are mostly selfish behaviors unfortunately. They are very harmful because these behaviors are particularly concerned with the interests of his own people, irrespective of the account that they damage other people and in some cases, exceptional people even die or huge damages are made.

1008. True friendship is tested in exceptionally difficult situations.

1009. Some successes are due only to the qualities and exceptional efforts of people without the participation of any favorable circumstances.

1010. In 2007, in most people in the world most behaviors are selfish behaviors unfortunately, they are very harmful ones because such behaviors are concerned with in particular, the interests of their own persons, irrespective of the fact that they often harm other people and in some exceptional cases people even die, or have huge damages.

1011. True friends are those who wish you well, cooperate with you when you need to, who are there by your side in every good and bad situation. They are those people who do not leave in exceptional circumstances, the most difficult ones of your life.

Experience

1012. The daily gathering of as much experience as possible helps us achieve more pleasant surprises.

1013. The daily gathering of as much experience as possible helps us achieve much good luck.

1014. The daily gathering of as much experience as possible helps us achieve more true friendships.

1015. The daily gathering of as much experience as possible helps us achieve more efficient co operations.

1016. The daily gathering of as much experience as possible helps us achieve more records.

1017. The daily gathering of as much experience as possible helps us achieve more personal goals.

1018. The daily gathering of as much experience as possible helps us achieve more favorable chances.

1019. Positive experience can be achieved also through the contribution of the formation, development, maintenance and usage of a behavior with a theoretic spirit.

1020. Positive experience can be achieved also through the contribution of the formation, development, maintenance and usage of bold behavior.

1021. Positive experience can be achieved also through the contribution of the formation, development, maintenance and usage of respectful behavior.

1022. Positive experience can be achieved also through the contribution of the formation, development, maintenance and usage of agreeable behavior.

1023. Positive experience can be achieved also through the contribution of the formation, development and maintenance of the ability to efficiently organize our time.

1024. By using experience we develop efficient collaborations.

1025. We can achieve objectives through experience.

1026. Failure can be prevented by taking as an example the experience of others.

1027. Positive experience can be achieved also through the contribution of the formation, development and maintenance of the ability to be calm in stressing situations.

1028. Positive experience can be achieved also through the contribution of the formation, development and maintenance of the ability to achieve efficient co operations.

1029. Positive experience can be achieved also through the contribution of the formation, development and maintenance of the ability to efficiently motivate people.

1030. The limits of achievement imposed by ourselves in our mind at a certain moment can be surpassed, eliminated also through the formation, development, maintenance and usage of the experience of people who have had successes.

1031. In order to change our desire of changing it is really necessary that we form, develop, maintain and use the ability to take as much as we need from other people's experience.

1032. In order to change our desire of changing it is really necessary that we form, develop, maintain and use the ability to willingly expand our experience.

1033. Positive experience can be achieved also through the contribution of the formation, development and maintenance of the ability to choose the road that fits us best in life.

1034. Positive experience can be achieved also through the contribution of the formation, development and maintenance of the ability to prevent mistakes.

1035. Our transformation for the better can be achieved also through the contribution of the formation, development, maintenance and usage of the ability to take what we need from other people's experience.

1036. A positive experience can be achieved also through the contribution of the formation, development and maintenance of the ability to solve problems only through positive methods.

1037. Our transformation for the better can be achieved also through the contribution of the formation, development, maintenance and usage of the ability to willingly expand our experience.

1038. We can prevent some failures also through the contribution of the formation, development, maintenance and usage of the ability to willingly expand our experience.

Failure

1039. Accomplishing exchanges of information helps us prevent many failures.

1040. An efficient man has fewer failures.

1041. A non hostile but aggressive behavior helps us a lot to prevent many failures.

1042. An organized man has fewer failures.

1043. An unrealistic man can have more failures.

1044. Prejudices create and contribute to producing more failures.

1045. Positive experience can be achieved also through the contribution of the formation, development and maintenance of the ability to prevent failures.

1046. Most of those who have not succeeded in building a happy marriage up to a certain date, in order to succeed they need to form and develop the ability to prevent failure.

1047. People who can control their emotions have a greater ability to prevent more possible failures.

1048. Constructive thinking avoids failures.

1049. The need to succeed contributes a lot to avoiding many failures.

1050. The sense of achieving quality in everything we do helps us a lot to prevent almost all the possible failures and even all of them because it is not impossible.

1051. People who have had successes in life have mostly had failures as well but they never let themselves be defeated by failures.

1052. Positive experience can be achieved also through the formation of the formation, development and maintenance of the ability to prevent failures.

1053. Our resistance to changing for the better can be defeated and surpassed also through the formation, development, maintenance and usage of the ability to prevent failures.

1054. Obtaining as many and great successes that we can can be achieved through the contribution of formation, development and maintenance of a great ability to prevent failures.

1055. Forming wrong ideas can be prevented through the contribution of the formation, development, maintenance and usage of the ability to prevent failures.

1056. We can prevent failures also through the contribution of the formation, development, maintenance and usage of the ability to efficiently organize our time.

1057. Hesitating behavior is the cause of many failures.

1058. Positive thinking helps us prevent many possible failures.

1059. A positive conception of life helps us a lot to prevent many failures.

1060. A man used to approach problems simultaneously from different points of view has greater chances to prevent more possible failures.

1061. The uncertainty of incomes may make us have more failures.

1062. Our choices influence enormously our success or failure.

1063. Hopes prevent many failures.

1064. Optimistic women have fewer failures in life.

1065. When spouses are optimistic they have more chances to have fewer failures in life.

1066. Love failures must never discourage us.

1067. Even if we have had many failures in achieving true friendships we must persevere until we succeed.

Facing

1068. A great capacity of facing one's own life must be a model.

1069. A great capacity of facing one's own life must be developed.

1070. A great capacity of facing one's own life helps us achieve more favorable chances.

1071. A great capacity of facing one's own life helps us maintain our way of being liked.

1072. In life, it is necessary to allow ourselves to be influenced only by positive influences, and when facing potential negative influences we must be immune.

1073. Those who have the ability of facing mental stress have more chances and a higher potential to achieve their desired future.

1074. A great capacity of facing one's own life helps us become more loved.

1075. A great capacity of facing one's own life helps us become practical.

1076. A great capacity of facing one's own life helps us maintain our tolerance.

1077. A great capacity of facing one's own life helps us maintain our happiness.

1078. A great capacity of facing one's own life helps us maintain our efficiency.

1079. A great capacity of facing one's own life helps us become more pleasant.

1080. A great capacity of facing one's own life helps us become more preventive.

1081. A great capacity of facing one's own life helps us maintain our way of being understanding.

Feelings

1082. When people reveal their feelings mutually they contribute a lot to maintaining inter-human relations.

1083. When friends reveal their feelings mutually they contribute a lot to maintaining a true friendship.

1084. Spouses must reveal their feelings mutually.

1085. Feelings must be rewarded with feelings.

1086. Feelings must be appreciated.

1087. Feelings must be expressed.

1088. Our happiness depends on the power to control our feelings.

1089. People who have had successes mostly have envious feelings.

1090. Each of us must have the strength and willpower to prevent negative feelings, to maintain and develop happiness because they are extremely harmful for us and for others.

1091. Negative feelings damage us and others. Attention not to make them, maintain and develop them.

1092. In life it is necessary and required to develop only positive feelings just because they only do us and others good.

1093. People who have deep feelings are also sensitive and profound.

1094. Each of us has the strength and will, if we want, to prevent the happiness, maintaining and development of negative feelings because they are extremely harmful to to us and others.

1095. Negative feelings harm both us and the others. Beware not to form, maintain and develop them.

1096. In life it is necessary and required to develop positive feelings just because they only do us and others good.

1097. By developing their inner beauty, the qualities, skills, abilities and feelings that make them happy, women can create more joy and satisfactions.

Flexibility

1098. Flexibility increases our chances of achieving more objectives.

1099. Flexibility increases our chances of achieving more successes.

1100. In order to transform positive objectives into reality it is necessary to form, develop, maintain and use the sense of flexibility.

1101. The limits we have set can be overcome by the formation, development, maintenance and usage of the sense of flexibility.

1102. Emancipation from restrictions can be made through the formation, development and maintenance of the sense of flexibility.

1103. Forming wrong ideas can be prevented also through the formation, development, maintenance and usage of flexibility.

1104. People who have had successes have the sense of flexibility.

1105. Those who have high objectives in life mostly have the sense of flexibility.

1106. Flexibility helps us a lot to increase our chances to achieve a more beautiful life.

1107. Flexibility increases our chances to achieve efficient co-developments.

1108. Flexibility helps us achieve much more efficient actions.

1109. Flexibility increases our possibilities to achieve our personal goals.

1110. Flexibility increases our chances to achieve more outstanding performances.

1111. Flexibility increases our chances of achieving true friendships.

1112. Flexibility helps us a lot to achieve more and greater successes.

1113. Flexibility increases our chances to meet more favorable situations.

1114. Flexibility in thinking and behaviors can be learned from those who have it.

1115. Flexibility in thinking and behaviors is a quality necessary to achieve personal goals.

1116. Flexibility in thinking and behaviors can be formed and developped if we do not have it.

1117. Flexibility in thinking and behaviors helps us surpass many hard to overcome obstacles.

1118. Flexibility in thinking and behavior helps us achieve much easier, much faster and a larger number of personal goals.

Focus

1119. Keeping the focus on achieving personal goals helps us achieve more successes.

1120. Keeping the focus on achieving personal goals helps us achieve more favorable chances.

1121. In order to pursue and transform our personal goals into reality we need to form, develop, maintain and use the ability to focus.

1122. Focusing on what we do helps us a lot to have even more chances to meet more favorable situations.

1123. The state of restlessness reduces a lot our ability to focus.

1124. Focusing on what we do helps us make the things we do of good quality.

1125. Focusing on what we do helps us a lot to achieve personal goals.

1126. When we focus on what we are doing we increase our chances to prevent mistakes.

1127. Focusing on what we do is a necessity.

1128. A nervous state reduces a lot our capacity to focus.

1129. The increased ability to focus our attention helps us contribute greatly to achieving more fulfillments.

1130. Increasing the ability to focus attention helps us and contributes to achieving independence.

1131. Increasing the ability to focus our attention helps contribute to the increasing of our efficiency in what we do.

1132. In life we may each receive more or less unjust blows. No unjust blow should consume us, because if we consume ourselves we do not solve anything but instead we harm us and sometimes even very much and we also complicate some problems that we have. First of all when we receive an unjust blow, we should focus on finding solutions, actions to help us minimize the negative effects of the blow, unless we can reduce them to zero.

Secondly, it is necessary to identify the causes and factors that led us to receiving them unjustly.

Thirdly, it is necessary to remove the causes that led us to receiving them unjustly, so that we shall not receive them again or several times again.

In the fourth line is necessary to take all necessary measures to prevent the causes that led us to reciving the X blow unjustly.

Fifthly it is necessary to seek to identify whether there are other causes that might lead us to receive further blows unjustly.

Sixthly it is necessary to discover other potential causes that could cause us to receive more unfair blows by taking the necessary measures: 1) to eliminate these causes, 2) where we can not prevent these causes it is necessary to take the necessary measures not to receive them unjustly, 3) if we receive them, to make the blow have as little negative effects as possible over us. In the seventh line it is necessary that our new situation caused by the unfair blow is used efficiently for us. It is possible that what we accomplish after the new situation created by the unjustly received blow is much larger and beneficial to us than the achievements that we had done if we had not received the blow unjustly.

1133. To achieve quality actions to become happy and maintain our happiness, it is necessary that every time we act to focus totally on that action, to be careful in everything we do. Any little distraction can have grater or smaller negative effects on our happiness. Because of this, our happiness totally depends on our overall happiness and on the quality of actions which we achieve, on the concentration and attention with which we perform them.

Friendship

1134. Preventing everything that harms women helps us achieve more true friendships.

1135. Preventing accidents helps us achieve more true friendships.

1136. Finding creative solutions to the problems helps us achieve more true friendships.

1137. The art of solving arguments helps us achieve more true friendships.

1138. Openness towards new solutions helps us achieve more true friendships.

1139. The power of hope helps us achieve more true friendships.

1140. The faithfulness of collaborators helps us achieve more true friendships.

1141. The attitude of not letting ourselves be stopped helps us achieve more true friendships.

1142. Passion for our work helps us achieve more true friendships.

1143. Imitating positive deeds helps us achieve more true friendships.

1144. The desire to be efficient helps us achieve more true friendships.

1145. Total concentration on personal goals helps us achieve more true friendships.

1146. Preventing failures helps us achieve more true friendships.

1147. Preventing everything that harms young people helps us achieve more true friendships.

1148. Useful ideas help us achieve more true friendships.

1149. Our positive attitude towards life helps us achieve more true friendships.

1150. Rising from more failures helps us achieve more true friendships.

1151. Preventing the inefficient use of resources helps us achieve more true friendships.

1152. Knowing about changes helps us achieve more true friendships.

1153. Those who have a good behavior help us achieve more true friendships.

1154. The power of continuous efficient organization helps us achieve more true friendships.

1155. The desire of achieving good deeds helps us achieve more true friendships.

1156. Preventing the inefficient use of financial resources helps us achieve more true friendships.

1157. Preventing everything that harms people helps us achieve more true friendships.

1158. The desire to accomplish positive deeds helps us achieve more true friendships.

1159. The daily gathering of as much experience as possible helps us achieve more true friendships.

1160. The power of continuously being effective helps us achieve more true friendships.

1161. Learning from other people's mistakes helps us achieve more true friendships.

1162. Gaining useful knowledge every day helps us achieve more true friendships.

Giving

1163. Never giving up helps us achieve more performances.

1164. Never giving up helps us achieve more favorable chances.

1165. Never giving up helps us achieve much good luck.

1166. Never giving up helps us achieve more personal goals.

1167. Forgiving is a wise behavior.

1168. Forgiving is a positive behavior.

1169. Very giving people, who are ready to interrupt their own way in order to help others, are an engine of global humanization.

1170. Very giving people, who are ready to interrupt their own way in order to help others, are an engine of development in each area of activity.

1171. People who are forgiving are also good.

1172. People who are forgiving are admired, esteemed, respected and rewarded.

1173. People who are forgiving manage to achieve true friendships.

1174. People who are forgiving know how to maintain a true mature love.

1175. Before giving an answer to a question it is necessary that one thinks about the answer and not give an answer without thinking.

1176. The majority of people who have successes are giving.

1177. By giving the attention and time necessary to nourish our souls we increase our chances to achieve personal goals.

1178. Very giving persons who are willing to interrupt their own way in order to help others, have greater chances to achieve efficient co operations.

1179. Maintaining a happy marriage is not done by itself automatically, but only by the giving and contribution of both spouses. Do not forget this principle and apply it, otherwise it is despair. Good luck.

1180. Mature love is due to the joining of the optimal intelligent rationality, accountability, realism and logic with pleasure, joy and mutual giving.

1181. True reciprocal giving of lovers is unique, not seen before, impossible to repeat, a totally special indescribable inexpressible fact.

1182. Very giving people ready to interrupt their own road to help others have the potential to become more efficient.

1183. Very giving people ready to interrupt their own road to help others have greater chances to achieve a more beautiful life.

Glad

1184. We must permanently be glad about other people's happiness.

1185. We must permanently be glad when we can help one or more persons.

1186. Some people are very glad when they succeed in developing their experience.

1187. Some people are glad when they succeed in developing their knowledge.

1188. Men need to be glad that women manage to have larger incomes than they do, because they have nothing to lose and should not have prejudices.

1189. Some of us are extremely glad when we manage to achieve a personal goal or more personal goals, and others have consumed their joys during their efforts in their work done to achieve that goal or those goals.

Goals

1190. Preventing conflicts helps us achieve more personal goals.

1191. The power of continuously being effective helps us achieve more personal goals.

1192. The passion of achieving personal goals helps us achieve more efficient co operations.

1193. Prevention against bad people helps us achieve more personal goals.

1194. The desire to become even more effective helps us achieve more personal goals.

1195. Preventing the inefficient use of the resources of informatics helps us achieve more personal goals.

1196. The passion of achieving personal goals helps us achieve much good luck.

1197. Keeping the focus on achieving personal goals helps us achieve more successes.

1198. Setting high personal goals helps us achieve more personal goals.

1199. Preventing inefficiencies helps us achieve more personal goals.

1200. Total concentration on personal goals helps us achieve more true friendships.

1201. Loving what we do helps us achieve more personal goals.

1202. Discovering true instincts helps us achieve more personal goals.

1203. The passion of achieving personal goals helps us achieve more pleasant surprises.

1204. Making problems aware helps us achieve more personal goals.

1205. Total concentration on personal goals helps us achieve more performances.

1206. Our loyalty helps us achieve more personal goals.

1207. The power of great dreams helps us achieve more personal goals.

1208. The power used to accomplish positive deeds helps us achieve more personal goals.

1209. The ability of achieving performances helps us achieve more personal goals.

1210. The will of going against everyone else's beliefs helps us achieve more personal goals.

1211. Knowing what is necessary for us to know helps us achieve more personal goals.

1212. The desire to accomplish records helps us achieve more personal goals.

1213. The passion of achieving personal goals helps us achieve more performances.

1214. Preventing negative behaviors helps us achieve more personal goals.

1215. Keeping the focus on achieving personal goals helps us achieve more favorable chances.

1216. Learning from other people's mistakes helps us achieve more personal goals.

1217. The ability to go against everybody's convictions helps us achieve more personal goals.

1218. Our everyday effective actions help us achieve more personal goals.

1219. Preventing worries helps us achieve more personal goals.

1220. Those who have a good behavior help us achieve more personal goals.

1221. The passion of achieving personal goals helps us achieve more favorable situations.

1222. The power to continuously efficiently organize things helps us achieve more personal goals.

1223. Imposing respect helps us achieve more personal goals.

1224. The desire to be better helps us achieve more personal goals.

1225. Imitating great minds helps us achieve more personal goals.

1226. The power of not allowing ourselves to be stopped helps us achieve more personal goals.

1227. Preventing everything that harms people helps us achieve more personal goals.

1228. The willpower of not allowing ourselves to be stopped helps us achieve more personal goals.

1229. Persevering in not letting ourselves be stopped helps us achieve more personal goals.

1230. The desire to accomplish positive deeds helps us achieve more personal goals.

1231. Finding creative solutions to the problems helps us achieve more personal goals.

Habits

1232. We must permanently form effective habits.

1233. Efficient habits help us achieve a happy life.

1234. Effective habits help us obtain our own successes.

1235. Positive habits can be developed continuously.

1236. We can form positive habits.

1237. Life is a lot easier if we have only positive habits.

1238. Those who fail to escape the routine of everyday habits have inefficient behavior, are messy, slow, chaotic, etc. and they will have many failures and few and small achievements in life.

1239. Routine and daily habits should not be a brake for us, an impassable barrier in the form of our other more efficient, more orderly, faster, etc. behaviors.

1240. Routine and daily habits should not be a brake for us, an impassable barrier in the form of our other more efficient, more orderly, faster, etc. behaviors

Happiness

1241. The desire to be grand helps us maintain our happiness.

1242. Our own happiness can be achieved and maintained also through the contribution of the formation, development, maintenance and usage of impersonal behavior.

1243. Our happiness depends a lot also on the formation, development, maintenance and usage of adaptable behavior.

1244. Our happiness depends a lot also on the formation, development, maintenance and usage of balanced behavior.

1245. Our happiness depends a lot also on the formation, development, maintenance and usage of analytic behavior.

1246. Our own happiness can be achieved and maintained also through the contribution of the formation, development, maintenance and usage of analytic behavior.

1247. Our own happiness can be achieved and maintained also through the contribution of the formation, development, maintenance and usage of charming behavior.

1248. Our happiness depends a lot also on the formation, development, maintenance and usage of joyful behavior.

1249. Our own happiness can be achieved and maintained also through the contribution of the formation, development, maintenance and usage of continuous self perfecting behavior.

1250. Our own happiness can be achieved and maintained also through the contribution of the formation, development, maintenance and usage of sensible behavior.

1251. A great capacity of being wise helps us maintain our happiness.

1252. Our happiness depends a lot also on the formation, development, maintenance and usage of conscientious behavior.

1253. Our own happiness can be achieved and maintained also through the contribution of the formation, development, maintenance and usage of self-controlled behavior.

1254. Our own happiness can be achieved and maintained also through the contribution of the formation, development, maintenance and usage of realistic behavior.

1255. Our happiness depends a lot also on the formation, development, maintenance and usage of scientific spirit behavior.

1256. Our own happiness can be achieved and maintained also through the contribution of the formation, development, maintenance and usage of a behavior of continuously efficiently using our time.

1257. Our happiness depends a lot also on the formation, development, maintenance and usage of selfless behavior.

1258. Our own happiness can be achieved and maintained also through the contribution of the formation, development, maintenance and usage of demanding behavior.

1259. Our happiness depends a lot also on the formation, development, maintenance and usage of a behavior of being eager for knowledge.

1260. Our own happiness can be achieved and maintained also through the contribution of the formation, development, maintenance and usage of fighting behavior.

1261. Our own happiness can be achieved and maintained also through the contribution of the formation, development, maintenance and usage of sportive behavior.

1262. A great capacity of being oneself helps us maintain our happiness.

1263. A great capacity of working hard helps us maintain our happiness.

1264. Our happiness depends a lot also on the formation, development, maintenance and usage of spontaneous behavior.

1265. A great capacity of continuously overcoming boundaries helps us maintain our happiness.

Harmonious

1266. When friends sense each other they have more chances to achieve harmonious relations.

1267. When people sense each other they have more chances to achieve harmonious relations.

1268. Those without hopes for the future need to become friends with those who harmoniously develop their personality.

1269. People who have had successes mostly know how to harmoniously develop their personality.

1270. Those who do not have hopes, in order to create hopes for the future they need to connect with people who have harmoniously developed their personality.

1271. Efficient positive human communication contributes a lot to achieving harmonious social relations.

1272. Those who are preoccupied with creating an optimal cooperation in the team contribute a lot to creating a harmonious climate.

1273. Working in teams of people with similar values is harmonious.

1274. A man who has practical values usually knows how to harmoniously develop his personality.

1275. A realistic man in everything he does knows how to harmoniously develop his personality.

1276. Correct relations with coworkers help us achieve more harmonious social relations.

1277. Those who are independent have the possibility to harmoniously develop their personality.

1278. A man with self control harmoniously develops his personality.

1279. Humanist economy will contribute a lot in the harmonious development of human personality.

1280. The economy of the harmonious development of human personality is an economy that is part of humanist economy.

1281. Humanist economy has the motivation to do good, to make a man happy, to offer him everything that he needs, to harmoniously develop his personality according to the surrounding environment.

Hope

1282. Release from self imposed restrictions can also be made through the formation, development and maintenance of hopes.

1283. People who do not have hopes, in order to create hopes need to connect with people who have the ability to face mental stress.

1284. Most of those involved in many projects have more hopes that increase their chances of participating in many efficient global co operations.

1285. Long term thinking creates many hopes.

1286. Most of those who have not succeeded in forming a happy marriage up to a certain date need to form and develop the abilities of creation, development and maintenance of hopes.

1287. Persons who do not have hopes, in order to create hopes for the future they need to connect with people who have the ability to take rapid decisions.

1288. People with no hopes for the future need to connect with those who have the ability of rapid perception.

1289. Those who do not have hopes, in order to create hopes for the future, they need to get themselves involved in relations with people who have the sense of fairness.

1290. Obtaining as many and great successes that we can, can be achieved through the contribution of formation, development, maintenance and usage of the ability to form, develop and maintain hopes.

1291. Aspirations toward a more meaningful life can be achieved also through the contribution of the formation, development, maintenance and usage of the ability to create, develop and maintain hopes.

1292. Emancipation from self imposed restrictions can be made through the formation, development and maintenance of hopes.

1293. The state of psychical discomfort can be removed through the formation, development and maintenance of hope.

1294. Our hopes are increased if we use optimistic thinking.

1295. Hopes have contributed a lot in achieving many successes.

1296. A man without hopes does not feel alive.

1297. Women's hopes make them feel alive.

1298. The hope of being happy must be encouraged.

1299. In order to rise up once again for the first time for the who knows what time it is necessary to also form, develop, maintain and use hopeful behavior.

1300. Hopes can be created also through the contribution of the formation, development, maintenance and usage of tolerant behavior.

1301. Obtaining more and greater successes can be achieved also through the contribution of the formation, development, maintenance, usage of a hopeful behavior.

1302. Rather than lamenting that we do not have successes it is more useful to also form, develop, maintain and use hopeful behavior.

1303. Hopes can be created also through the contribution of the formation, development, maintenance and usage of spiritual behavior.

1304. In order to escape poverty it is necessary to also form, develop, maintain and use hopeful behavior.

1305. We can form, develop and maintain the state of being ourselves also through the contribution of the formation, development, maintenance and usage of a hopeful behavior.

1306. Hopes can be created also through the contribution of the formation, development, maintenance and usage of a behavior of continuous self-motivation.

Honest

1307. A great capacity of being honest with oneself helps us achieve more favorable chances.

1308. A great capacity of being honest with oneself helps us become more practical.

1309. A great capacity of being honest with oneself helps us maintain our way of being loving.

1310. A great capacity of being honest with oneself helps us become happier.

1311. A great capacity of being honest with oneself helps us maintain our tolerance.

1312. A great capacity of being honest with oneself helps us maintain our way of being liked.

1313. A great capacity of being honest with oneself helps us become more efficient.

1314. A great capacity of being honest with oneself helps us achieve more personal goals.

1315. A great capacity of being honest with oneself helps us achieve more performances. A great capacity of being honest with oneself helps us become enthusiastic.

1316. A great capacity of being honest with oneself helps us become efficient.

1317. In order to follow and transform our personal goals into reality, it is necessary to also form, develop, maintain and use our honest behavior.

1318. True friendships rely on honesty.

1319. Honesty demands honesty.

1320. An honest woman has more chances to achieve a happy marriage.

1321. Troubles can be prevented through using honest behaviors.

1322. People who have had successes are mostly honest.

1323. An honest man manages to earn his living in life.

1324. An honest man works hard all the time.

1325. Honest men must be promoted, supported, appreciated.

1326. An honest man is consistent in honest behaviors.

1327. Those who are very honest are much appreciated.
1328. An honest man is appreciated, respected and esteemed by other people.

1329. Honesty brings us luck.

1330. Those who establish as an objective to be honest and continuously act with commitment to achieve this objective will be honest.

Himself

1331. Honesty is a quality that prevents many misdoings.

1332. A vigilant man has more chances to perfect himself.

1333. The optimistic man has more chances to surpass himself.

1334. A man who knows how to protect himself continuously makes exchanges of ideas.

1335. A man sure of himself most of the times knows how to efficiently manage his time.

1336. A man who knows how to protect himself is resistant to stress.

1337. A man with tactical values accomplishes himself in life.

1338. A man sure of himself has great possibilities to achieve outstanding performances.

1339. An open man has much more chances to achieve a happy life for himself.

1340. A man with a good imagination of himself has a greater confidence in himself.

1341. A man's need to achieve himself has continuously contributed to increasing the efficiency of human actions.

1342. A man who knows how to protect himself can prevent many mistakes.

1343. A man sure of himself more easily achieves true friendships.

1344. A conscious man changes his life for the better by himself.

1345. A man who knows how to protect himself permanently takes preventive measures.

1346. A man sure of himself has much more and greater chances to meet more favorable situations.

1347. A man who knows how to protect himself has thrust in himself.

1348. A man sure of himself has great chances of achieving efficient co-developments.

1349. A reliable man has the potential to help himself achieve a happy life.

1350. He who is sure of himself has more chances to face stressing situations.

1351. He who says unconsidered words can many times harm others too, not only himself.

1352. He who says unconsidered words many times harms himself.

1353. Man's need to achieve himself has contributed greatly to achieving the greater good.

1354. A man who knows how to protect himself must know how to choose his friends.

1355. A man sure of himself has great chances to achieve a more beautiful life.

Honorable

1356. Perseverant people are honorable.

1357. Perseverance gives us power, strenghtens us, makes us honorable, respected and appreciated.

1358. People with successes are honorable.

Humanity

1359. A great capacity of analyzing a situation logically helps us maintain our humanity.

1360. A great capacity of working hard helps us maintain our humanity.

1361. A great capacity of fighting back helps us maintain our humanity.

1362. A great capacity of maintaining relationships with people helps us maintain our humanity.

1363. The desire to be grand helps us maintain our humanity.

1364. A great capacity of cherishing oneself helps us maintain our humanity.

1365. A great capacity of investing efficiently helps us maintain our humanity.

1366. A great capacity of continuously enhancing performances helps us maintain our humanity.

1367. A great capacity of adopting visions helps us maintain our humanity.

1368. A great capacity of increasing creativity helps us maintain our humanity.

1369. A great capacity of doing what is best helps us maintain our humanity.

1370. A great capacity of using each failure to achieve successes helps us maintain our humanity.

1371. A great capacity of creating one's own safety helps us maintain our humanity.

1372. A great capacity of using available ideas helps us maintain our humanity.

1373. A great capacity of being popular helps us maintain our humanity.

1374. A great capacity of maintaining a positive efficient own lifestyle helps us maintain our humanity.

1375. A great capacity of using qualities helps us maintain our humanity.

1376. A great capacity of assuming the necessary risks for achieving great successes helps us maintain our humanity.

1377. A great capacity of establishing great personal goals helps us maintain our humanity.

1378. A great capacity of facing one's own life helps us maintain our humanity.

1379. A great capacity of rapid instruction helps us maintain our humanity.

1380. A great capacity of remaining involved in the same area with even greater objectives helps us maintain our humanity.

1381. A great capacity of using each personal mistake to achieve successes helps us maintain our humanity.

1382. The dream to the grand helps us maintain our humanity.

1383. A great capacity of self-surpassing helps us maintain our humanity.

Hypocrisy

1384. Hypocrisy harms the hypocrite one very much.

1385. Hypocrisy makes those who are hypocrites be rejected by others.

1386. A strong man by his hypocrisy enormously damages himself due to his hypocrisy.

1387. He who is hypocritical only has common sense to achieve his hypocrisy.

1388. Hypocrisy only creates problems and nothing positive.

1389. Hypocrisy alienates others from the hypocritical one.

1390. Hypocrisy is extremely dangerous.

1391. He who is hypocrite through his hypocrisy enormously harms himself because of his hypocrisy.

1392. The hypocrisy of a friend towards the other leads to the destruction of the friendship.

1393. Hypocrisy can not be found between two friends.

1394. Hypocrisy is a defect that harms people very much.

1395. Hypocrisy is a big flaw that harms us very much in life.

Ideals

1396. Our life's transformation for the better can be achieved if we have ideals.

1397. People with high ideals have much greater chances of achieving efficient co operations.

1398. Those who are remarkably gifted mostly have a lot of ideals.

Immorality

1399. Immorality is a question of many misfortunes.

1400. Immorality is a factor of many failures.

1401. Immorality undermines the very immoral one.

1402. Immorality makes the immoral ones be rejected by others.

1403. Immorality is enormously harmful to society.

Ignorance

1404. Ignorance can be fought by using discipline.

1405. Our ignorance can be removed by progressive conceptions of life.

1406. Our remaining in ignorance can be eliminated also through the contribution of the formation, development, maintenance and usage of progressive ideas.

1407. Our remaining in ignorance can be eliminated also through the contribution of the formation, development, maintenance and usage of a constructive conception of life.

1408. Ignorance can be avoided through creativity and study.

1409. Our remaining in ignorance can be removed also through the contribution of the formation, development, maintenance and usage of a positive life conception.

1410. Our remaining in ignorance can be removed also through the contribution of the formation, development, maintenance and usage of creative sense.

1411. Our remaining in ignorance can be removed also through the contribution of the formation, development, maintenance and usage of a legal conception of life.

1412. Our remaining in ignorance can be removed also through the contribution of the formation, development, maintenance and usage of the ability to make the positive necessary changes in our personal life.

1413. Our remaining in ignorance can be removed also through the contribution of the formation, development, maintenance and usage of an efficient conception of life.

1414. Our remaining in ignorance can be removed also through the contribution of the formation, development, maintenance and usage of a constructive conception of life.

1415. Our remaining in ignorance can be removed also through the contribution of the formation, development, maintenance and usage of a realistic life conception.

1416. Our remaining in ignorance can be removed also through the contribution of the formation, development, maintenance and usage of progressive ideas.

1417. Our remaining in ignorance can be removed also through the contribution of the formation, development, maintenance and usage of a constructive life conception.

1418. Our remaining in ignorance can be removed also through the contribution of the formation, development, maintenance and usage of scientific thinking.

1419. Remaining in a state of ignorance can be fought through the contribution of the formation, development, maintenance and usage of a positive life conception.

1420. Ignorance is the cause of many failures.

1421. Ignorance is a cause of pessimism.

1422. Ignorance is the cause of many divorces.

1423. Ignorance is the cause of many mistakes.

1424. Ignorance is the cause of many arguments.

1425. Ignorance also produces envy.

1426. Ignorance produces much evil.

1427. Meanness is a result of ignorance.

1428. Sometimes ignorance makes our life very complicated.

Indecision

1429. Indecision can sometimes harm us very much.

1430. When we are doubtful we must find solutions to get rid of indecision.

1431. Indecision is the cause of many casualties.

1432. Indecision is the cause of many accidents.

1433. Indecision is the cause of many failures.

Inefficinent

1434. Preventing the inefficient use of the resources of informatics helps us achieve more efficient co operations.

1435. Preventing the inefficient use of financial resources helps us achieve much good luck.

1436. Preventing the inefficient use of the resources of informatics helps us achieve more personal goals.

1437. Preventing the inefficient use of human resources helps us achieve more records.

1438. Preventing the inefficient use of financial resources helps us achieve more successes.

1439. Preventing the inefficient use of material resources helps us achieve much good luck.

1440. Preventing the inefficient use of resources helps us achieve more true friendships.

1441. Preventing the inefficient use of financial resources helps us achieve more true friendships.

1442. Preventing the inefficient use of financial resources helps us achieve more records.

1443. Preventing the inefficient use of the resources of informatics helps us achieve more favorable chances.

1444. Preventing the inefficient use of the resources of informatics helps us achieve more performances.

1445. Preventing the inefficient use of material resources helps us achieve more personal goals.

1446. Preventing the inefficient use of resources helps us achieve more successes.

1447. Preventing the inefficient use of human resources helps us achieve more favorable chances.

1448. Preventing the inefficient use of financial resources helps us achieve more personal goals.

Influence

1449. A great capacity of having one's own principles and not letting one be influenced by the negative opinions of others helps us maintain our way of being cautious.

1450. We can become stronger and we can not allow ourselves to be influenced by the world also through the contribution of the formation, development, maintenance and usage of sturdy behavior.

1451. We can become stronger and we can not allow ourselves to be influenced by the world also through the contribution of the formation, development, maintenance and usage of ingenious behavior.

1452. We can become stronger and we can not allow ourselves to be influenced by the world also through the contribution of the formation, development, maintenance and usage of astute behavior.

1453. We can become stronger and we can not allow ourselves to be influenced by the world also through the contribution of the formation, development, maintenance and usage of daring behavior.

1454. A great capacity of having one's own principles and not letting one be influenced by the negative opinions of others helps us maintain our optimism.

1455. We can become stronger and we can not allow ourselves to be influenced by the world also through the contribution of the formation, development, maintenance and usage of diplomatic behavior.

1456. We can become stronger and we can not allow ourselves to be influenced by the world also through the contribution of the formation, development, maintenance and usage of idealistic behavior.

1457. A great capacity of having one's own principles and not letting one be influenced by the negative opinions of others helps us become practical.

1458. We can become stronger and we can not allow ourselves to be influenced by the world also through the contribution of the formation, development, maintenance and usage of productive behavior.

1459. We can become stronger and we can not allow ourselves to be influenced by the world also through the contribution of the formation, development, maintenance and usage of profound behavior.

1460. A great capacity of having one's own principles and not letting one be influenced by the negative opinions of others must be encouraged.

1461. A great capacity of having one's own principles and not letting one be influenced by the negative opinions of others helps us become more loving.

1462. A great capacity of having one's own principles and not letting one be influenced by the negative opinions of others helps us become more tolerant.

1463. A great capacity of having one's own principles and not letting one be influenced by the negative opinions of others helps us become more enthusiastic.

1464. A great capacity of having one's own principles and not letting one be influenced by the negative opinions of others helps us maintain our way of being understanding.

1465. We can become stronger and we can not allow ourselves to be influenced by the world also through the contribution of the formation, development, maintenance and usage of ordered behavior.

1466. We can become stronger and we can not allow ourselves to be influenced by the world also through the contribution of the formation, development, maintenance and usage of sociable behavior.

1467. A great capacity of having one's own principles and not letting one be influenced by the negative opinions of others helps us become tolerant.

1468. A great capacity of having one's own principles and not letting one be influenced by the negative opinions of others helps us achieve more true friendships.

1469. We can become stronger and we can not allow ourselves to be influenced by the world also through the contribution of the formation, development, maintenance and usage of sincere behavior.

Ingenuity

1470. Ingenuity must be recognized.

1471. Ingenuity must be appreciated.

1472. Ingenuity is a creative quality.

1473. Our ingenuity helps us create and maintain a happy family.

Initiatives

1474. Assuming initiatives helps us achieve much good luck.

1475. Assuming initiatives helps us achieve more favorable situations.

1476. Assuming initiatives helps us achieve more favorable chances.

1477. Assuming initiatives helps us achieve more successes.

1478. Assuming initiatives helps us achieve more records.

1479. Assuming initiatives helps us achieve more personal goals.

1480. Assuming initiatives helps us achieve more pleasant surprises.

1481. Assuming initiatives helps us achieve more true friendships.

1482. The financing by the state of more positive, efficient initiatives, helpful to people and society should contribute a lot and would accelerate the development of their personality, their integration into society, from participating in the realization of many activities of society.

1483. The state's funding of more positive and effective initiatives, useful for the youth and for society would greatly reduce the number of young negative facts.

1484. Countries should promote, encourage and finance more positive and effective initiatives of young people.

Innovating

1485. People with an innovating spirit have a great potential to participate in efficient global co operations.

1486. People with and innovating spirit have much more chances to meet more favorable situations.

1487. People with an innovating spirit more easily achieve efficient co operations.

1488. People with an innovating spirit more easily achieve social relations.

1489. People who have an innovating spirit have more potential to find the right partner for life.

1490. People who have and innovating spirit have more potential to increase their efficiency.

Intelectual

1491. The force of our ideas can be augmented also through the contribution of the formation, development, maintenance and usage of intellectual behavior.

1492. We can prevent the falling apart of a happy marriage also through the contribution of the formation, development, maintenance and usage of intellectual behavior.

1493. Our future can be projected and achieved also through the contribution of the formation, development, maintenance and usage of intellectual behavior.

1494. In order to prevent not achieving our personal goals, it is necessary to also form, develop, maintain and use our intellectual behavior.

1495. Acting efficiently helps us become intellectual.

1496. The radical transformation for the better of our life can be achieved also through the formation, development, maintenance and usage of intellectual behavior.

1497. In order to escape poverty it is necessary to also form, develop, maintain and use intellectual behavior.

1498. Positive experience can be achieved also through the contribution of the formation, development, maintenance and usage of intellectual behavior.

1499. Our own happiness can be achieved and maintained also through the contribution of the formation, development, maintenance and usage of intellectual behavior.

1500. Stress can be prevented also through the formation, development, maintenance and usage of intellectual behavior.

1501. We can overcome the difficulties that we must overcome also through the help of the formation, development, maintenance and usage of intellectual behavior.

1502. The obstacles that prevent us from achieving our personal goals can be surpassed also through the contribution of the formation, development, maintenance and usage of intellectual behavior.

1503. We can form, develop and maintain the state of being ourselves also through the contribution of the formation, development, maintenance and usage of an intellectual behavior.

1504. Our resistance to changing for the better can be overcome also through the contribution of the formation, development, maintenance and usage of intellectual behavior.

1505. In order to prevent failures it is necessary to also form, develop, maintain and use intellectual behavior.

1506. The limits of achievement imposed by ourselves in our mind at a given moment can be overcome or eliminated also through the contribution of the formation, development, maintenance and usage of intellectual behavior.

1507. Rather than lamenting that we do not have successes it is more useful to also form, develop, maintain and use intellectual behavior.

1508. Pessimism can be removed and replaced with optimism also through the contribution of the formation, development, maintenance and usage of intellectual behavior.

1509. Problems cannot be solved by the ideas that created them but also through the contribution of the formation, development, maintenance and usage of intellectual behavior.

1510. Aspiring towards a more meaningful life can also be achieved through the formation, development, maintenance and usage of intellectual behavior.

1511. Hopes can be created also through the contribution of the formation, development, maintenance and usage of intellectual behavior.

1512. We can become stronger and we can not allow ourselves to be influenced by the world also through the contribution of the formation, development, maintenance and usage of intellectual behavior.

1513. Self-imposed discipline helps us become intellectual.

1514. Our happiness depends a lot also on the formation, development, maintenance and usage of intellectual behavior.

1515. Release from our self-imposed restrictions can be made also through the contribution of the formation, development, maintenance and usage of intellectual behavior.

Irresponsability

1516. Unfortunately there are still enormously many people in functions with high responsibilities but who unfortunately prove much irresponsibility.

1517. After a while, when they are divorced, they realize their irresponsibility, the enormous value that they had lost and that their children had lost.

1518. Leaders of countries have an enormous responsibility to the people, but unfortunately they often demonstrate very much and great irresponsibility.

1519. All employees of international organizations and states, which act during the performance of their duties with irresponsibility should be dismissed immediately and effective measures to recover the damage created by their irresponsible actions should be taken.

1520. The irresponsibility of many people stopped in a lot of ways until now, progress in many areas.

Jealousy

1521. The self-control of our behaviors helps us a lot to prevent jealousy.

1522. Causing jealousy to a husband or wife is one of the biggest human stupidities.

1523. Both the wife and husband should not provoke jealousy to each other because this can harm them enormously much in certain situations, and even lead to divorce, to arguments and continuous conflict, unbearable tension which could lead to divorce.

Joyful

1524. Our future can be projected and achieved also through the contribution of the formation, development, maintenance and usage of joyful behavior.

1525. We can form, develop and maintain the state of being ourselves also through the contribution of the formation, development, maintenance and usage of a joyful behavior.

1526. The radical transformation for the better of our life can be achieved also through the formation, development, maintenance and usage of joyful behavior.

1527. Our happiness depends a lot also on the formation, development, maintenance and usage of joyful behavior.

1528. Problems cannot be solved by the ideas that created them but also through the contribution of the formation, development, maintenance and usage of joyful behavior.

1529. We can contribute to the achievement of our greatest accomplishments also through the contribution of the formation, development, maintenance and usage of joyful behavior.

1530. Continuously making ourselves efficient helps us become joyful.

1531. In order to escape poverty it is necessary to also form, develop, maintain and use joyful behavior.

1532. Hopes can be created also through the contribution of the formation, development, maintenance and usage of joyful behavior.

1533. The force of our ideas can be augmented also through the contribution of the formation, development, maintenance and usage of joyful behavior.

1534. Our own happiness can be achieved and maintained also through the contribution of the formation, development, maintenance and usage of joyful behavior.

1535. We can prevent the falling apart of a happy marriage also through the contribution of the formation, development, maintenance and usage of joyful behavior.

1536. Continuous self perfection helps us become joyful.

1537. In achieving our successes a contribution is also brought by the formation, development, maintenance and usage of joyful behavior.

1538. Aspiring towards a more meaningful life can also be achieved through the formation, development, maintenance and usage of joyful behavior.

1539. We can overcome the difficulties that we must overcome also through the help of the formation, development, maintenance and usage of joyful behavior.

1540. Self-imposed discipline helps us become joyful.

1541. The obstacles that prevent us from achieving our personal goals can be surpassed also through the contribution of the formation, development, maintenance and usage of joyful behavior.

1542. Release from our self-imposed restrictions can be made also through the contribution of the formation, development, maintenance and usage of joyful behavior.

1543. Confidence in ourselves helps us become joyful.

1544. Will helps us become joyful.

1545. Obtaining more and greater successes can be achieved also through the contribution of the formation, development, maintenance, usage of a joyful behavior.

1546. Continuous self-motivation helps us become joyful.

1547. The solutions to the problems we have or that we want to solve can be found also through the contribution of the formation, development, maintenance and usage of joyful behavior.

1548. Optimism helps us become joyful.

1549. The necessary qualities in achieving personal goals can be formed, developed, maintained and used also through the contribution of the formation, development, maintenance and usage of joyful behavior.

1550. Rather than lamenting that we do not have successes it is more useful to also form, develop, maintain and use joyful behavior.

1551. Our resistance to changing for the better can be overcome also through the contribution of the formation, development, maintenance and usage of joyful behavior.

1552. In order to rise up once again for the first time for the who knows what time it is necessary to also form, develop, maintain and use joyful behavior.

1553. The limits of achievement imposed by ourselves in our mind at a given moment can be overcome or eliminated also through the contribution of the formation, development, maintenance and usage of joyful behavior.

1554. We can become stronger and we can not allow ourselves to be influenced by the world also through the contribution of the formation, development, maintenance and usage of joyful behavior.

1555. Pessimism can be removed and replaced with optimism also through the contribution of the formation, development, maintenance and usage of joyful behavior.

1556. In order to prevent not achieving our personal goals, it is necessary to also form, develop, maintain and use our joyful behavior.

1557. Some mistakes can be prevented also through the contribution of the formation, development, maintenance and usage of joyful behavior.

1558. In order to prevent failures it is necessary to also form, develop, maintain and use joyful behavior.

1559. Stress can be prevented also through the formation, development, maintenance and usage of joyful behavior.

1560. Positive experience can be achieved also through the contribution of the formation, development, maintenance and usage of joyful behavior.

1561. In order to follow and transform our personal goals into reality, it is necessary to also form, develop, maintain and use our joyful behavior.

Kind

1562. Continuous self-control helps us become kind.

1563. In order to rise up once again for the first time for the who knows what time it is necessary to also form, develop, maintain and use kind behavior.

1564. In order to rise up once again for the first time for the who knows what time it is necessary to also form, develop, maintain and use kind behavior.

1565. Optimism helps us become kind.

1566. Will helps us become kind.

1567. The self efficient use of our time helps us become kind.

1568. The force of our ideas can be augmented also through the contribution of the formation, development, maintenance and usage of kind behavior.

1569. We can form, develop and maintain the state of being ourselves also through the contribution of the formation, development, maintenance and usage of a kind behavior.

1570. Problems cannot be solved by the ideas that created them but also through the contribution of the formation, development, maintenance and usage of kind behavior.

1571. Wisdom helps us become kind.

1572. Some mistakes can be prevented also through the contribution of the formation, development, maintenance and usage of kind behavior.

1573. Positive experience can be achieved also through the contribution of the formation, development, maintenance and usage of kind behavior.

1574. We can overcome the difficulties that we must overcome also through the help of the formation, development, maintenance and usage of kind behavior.

1575. Stress can be prevented also through the formation, development, maintenance and usage of kind behavior.

1576. Pessimism can be removed and replaced with optimism also through the contribution of the formation, development, maintenance and usage of kind behavior.

1577. The solutions to the problems we have or that we want to solve can be found also through the contribution of the formation, development, maintenance and usage of kind behavior.

1578. Acting efficiently helps us become kind.

1579. Release from our self-imposed restrictions can be made also through the contribution of the formation, development, maintenance and usage of kind behavior.

1580. Our own happiness can be achieved and maintained also through the contribution of the formation, development, maintenance and usage of kind behavior.

1581. Rather than lamenting that we do not have successes it is more useful to also form, develop, maintain and use kind behavior.

Kindness

1582. In order to follow and transform our personal goals into reality, it is necessary to also form, develop, maintain and use our kindness.

1583. Kindness must never lack.

Knowledge

1584. The daily gathering of as much useful knowledge as possible helps us achieve more efficient co operations.

1585. Gaining useful knowledge every day helps us achieve more records.

1586. The daily gathering of as much useful knowledge as possible helps us achieve more performances.

1587. The daily gathering of as much useful knowledge as possible helps us achieve much good luck.

1588. Gaining useful knowledge every day helps us achieve much good luck.

1589. The daily gathering of as much useful knowledge as possible helps us achieve more records.

1590. The daily gathering of as much useful knowledge as possible helps us achieve more pleasant surprises.

1591. Gaining useful knowledge every day helps us achieve more pleasant surprises.

1592. The daily gathering of as much useful knowledge as possible helps us achieve more favorable chances.

1593. Gaining useful knowledge every day helps us achieve more successes.

1594. The daily gathering of as much useful knowledge as possible helps us achieve more favorable situations.

1595. The daily gathering of as much useful knowledge as possible helps us achieve more successes.

1596. The daily gathering of as much useful knowledge as possible helps us achieve more personal goals.

1597. Gaining useful knowledge every day helps us achieve more favorable chances.

1598. Gaining useful knowledge every day helps us achieve more performances.

1599. The daily gathering of as much useful knowledge as possible helps us achieve more true friendships.

1600. A great capacity of using available knowledge helps us become more efficient.

1601. Release from our self-imposed restrictions can be made also through the contribution of the formation, development, maintenance and usage of a behavior eager for knowledge.

1602. A great capacity of using available knowledge helps us become more cautious.

1603. Our happiness depends a lot also on the formation, development, maintenance and usage of a behavior of being eager for knowledge.

1604. We can overcome the difficulties that we must overcome also through the help of the formation, development, maintenance and usage of a behavior of being eager for knowledge.

1605. Acting efficiently helps us become eager for knowledge.

1606. Problems cannot be solved by the ideas that created them but also through the contribution of the formation, development, maintenance and usage of a behavior of being eager for knowledge.

1607. Obtaining more and greater successes can be achieved also through the contribution of the formation, development, maintenance, usage of a behavior eager for knowledge.

1608. In order to prevent not achieving our personal goals, it is necessary to also form, develop, maintain and use our behavior of being eager for knowledge.

1609. A great capacity of using available knowledge helps us become understanding.

1610. Our resistance to changing for the better can be overcome also through the contribution of the formation, development, maintenance and usage of a behavior eager for knowledge.

1611. Aspiring towards a more meaningful life can also be achieved through the formation, development, maintenance and usage of a behavior of being eager for knowledge.

1612. A great capacity of using available knowledge helps us maintain our efficiency.

1613. A great capacity of using available knowledge helps us become practical.

1614. A great capacity of using available knowledge helps us maintain our productivity.

1615. A great capacity of using available knowledge must be maintained.

1616. Positive experience can be achieved also through the contribution of the formation, development, maintenance and usage of a behavior eager for knowledge.

1617. In achieving our successes a contribution is also brought by the formation, development, maintenance and usage of a behavior of being eager for knowledge.

1618. In order to rise up once again for the first time for the who knows what time it is necessary to also form, develop, maintain and use a behavior of being eager for knowledge.

1619. We can prevent the falling apart of a happy marriage also through the contribution of the formation, development, maintenance and usage of a behavior eager for knowledge.

1620. A great capacity of using available knowledge helps us achieve more true friendships.

1621. We can prevent some failures also through the contribution of the formation, development, maintenance and usage of a behavior of being eager for knowledge.

1622. Our future can be projected and achieved also through the contribution of the formation, development, maintenance and usage of a behavior of being eager for knowledge.

1623. Self-imposed discipline helps us become eager for knowledge.

1624. A great capacity of using available knowledge helps us become productive.

1625. We can form, develop and maintain the state of being ourselves also through the contribution of the formation, development, maintenance and usage of a behavior eager for knowledge.

1626. A great capacity of using available knowledge helps us achieve more successes.

1627. A great capacity of using available knowledge helps us maintain our way of being liked.

1628. We can contribute to the achievement of our greatest accomplishments also through the contribution of the formation, development, maintenance and usage of a behavior eager for knowledge.

1629. Some mistakes can be prevented also through the contribution of the formation, development, maintenance and usage of a behavior eager for knowledge.

1630. The radical transformation for the better of our life can be achieved also through the formation, development, maintenance and usage of a behavior of being eager for knowledge.

1631. A great capacity of using available knowledge helps us maintain our humanity.

Laziness

1632. Laziness brings only suffering.

1633. Laziness stops those who are lazy from getting a job.

1634. Laziness makes many people poor.

1635. Laziness is a dangerous defect.

1636. Laziness a dangerous defect.

1637. Laziness has never led to the achievement of any success.

1638. Laziness makes people who are lazy be put on the lists of dismissals.

1639. Laziness has never led to anything.

1640. Laziness of one of the spouses is likely to lead to divorce.

1641. Laziness is a cause of poverty for many poor people.

1642. Laziness also makes us even poorer.

1643. Laziness leads us to poverty.

Learning

1644. Learning from other people's mistakes helps us achieve more favorable situations.

1645. Learning how to solve problems helps us achieve more records.

1646. Learning how to solve problems helps us achieve much good luck.

1647. Learning from other people's mistakes helps us achieve more successes.

1648. Learning how to solve problems helps us achieve more performances.

1649. A great capacity of learning how to achieve personal goals helps us achieve more performances.

1650. A great capacity of learning in order to achieve successes helps us maintain our optimism.

1651. A great capacity of learning in order to achieve successes must be supported.

1652. A great capacity of learning how to achieve personal goals helps us become productive.

1653. A great capacity of learning in order to achieve successes helps us achieve more personal goals.

1654. A great capacity of learning how to achieve personal goals must be maintained.

1655. A great capacity of learning how to achieve personal goals must be rewarded.

1656. A great capacity of learning how to achieve personal goals helps us become practical.

1657. A great capacity of learning how to achieve personal goals helps us maintain our tolerance.

1658. A great capacity of learning how to achieve personal goals helps us maintain our efficiency.

1659. A great capacity of learning how to achieve personal goals must be developed.

1660. The quality of learning effectively must be formed if we do not have it.

1661. Self-imposed discipline can be obtained through experiences, through practice, through imitating, through learning, etc.

1662. The quality of learning how to learn helps us form the abilities we lead to achieve our personal goals.

1663. The quality of learning how to learn increases our chances to be more efficient.

1664. The quality of learning how to learn helps us become more operative.

1665. The quality of learning how to learn contributes a lot in maintaining some efficient co operations.

1666. The ability of learning how to learn increases our chances of achieving a more beautiful life.

1667. The ability of learning how to learn increases our chances to meet more favorable situations.

1668. The capacity of learning how to learn helps us achieve our personal goals much easier.

1669. Learning and applying strategies of achieving happiness do not require many efforts but many people do almost nothing to learn and apply them although they may help create their own happiness.

Long-term

1670. The effects of human actions have an increasing influence on the environment. This makes us think on a global scale, long-term and scientific before acting and makes us perform more profound studies, of impact, regarding our actions, to prevent the implementation of actions that have negative, inadmissible effects on the environment, society and people.

1671. To have the least possible number of failures in our life it is also necessary to have a long-term thinking.

1672. We can prevent many failures can with the help of long-term thinking.

1673. Thinking long-term helps us to prevent many mistakes.

1674. We can prevent a very large number of inefficient actions with a long-term thinking.

1675. Incredible facts are made mostly by people who have long-term objectives and work with dedication to achieve them.

1676. Short-term thinking is necessary to be combined with long-term thinking.

1677. The great and special achievements of mankind have been carried out by people who have used long-term thinking.

1678. It is necessary and required that society develops studies and research about the future, thinking futurologically, long-term projects for faster implementation and development of some theories, a more complete knowledge of them to be able to handle projects for the future and prevent mistakes made previously by society.

1679. Long-term thinking is specific to futurological thinking.

1680. Hopes make us form our long-term thinking.

1681. Thinking long-term helps and contributes greatly to increasing our confidence in us.

1682. A man with a broad horizon most of the times has a long-term thinking.

1683. People with human social behaviors have a long-term thinking.

1684. People with no hopes for the future need to connect with those who have a long-term thinking.

1685. In order to escape poverty it is necessary to form, develop, maintain and use long-term thinking.

1686. Hopes can be created by using a long-term thinking.

Mannered

1687. In order to prevent failures it is necessary to also form, develop, maintain and use mannered behavior.

1688. Continuous self perfection helps us become mannered.

1689. Our own happiness can be achieved and maintained also through the contribution of the formation, development, maintenance and usage of mannered behavior.

1690. The solutions to the problems we have or that we want to solve can be found also through the contribution of the formation, development, maintenance and usage of mannered behavior.

1691. The obstacles that prevent us from achieving our personal goals can be surpassed also through the contribution of the formation, development, maintenance and usage of mannered behavior.

1692. We can form, develop and maintain the state of being ourselves also through the contribution of the formation, development, maintenance and usage of a mannered behavior.

1693. In order to escape poverty it is necessary to also form, develop, maintain and use mannered behavior.

1694. The force of our ideas can be augmented also through the contribution of the formation, development, maintenance and usage of mannered behavior.

1695. Communication helps us become mannered.

1696. Our future can be projected and achieved also through the contribution of the formation, development, maintenance and usage of mannered behavior.

1697. Pessimism can be removed and replaced with optimism also through the contribution of the formation, development, maintenance and usage of mannered behavior.

1698. Rather than lamenting that we do not have successes it is more useful to also form, develop, maintain and use mannered behavior.

1699. Wisdom helps us become mannered.

1700. In order to rise up once again for the first time for the who knows what time it is necessary to also form, develop, maintain and use mannered behavior.

1701. The limits of achievement imposed by ourselves in our mind at a given moment can be overcome or eliminated also through the contribution of the formation, development, maintenance and usage of mannered behavior.

1702. Hope helps us become mannered.

Misunderstandings

1703. The ability to solve misunderstandings helps us achieve more pleasant surprises.

1704. Finding creative solutions that contribute to solving misunderstandings helps us achieve more true friendships.

1705. The art of solving misunderstandings helps us achieve more true friendships.

Model

1706. A great capacity of making great plans must be a model.

1707. A great capacity of adopting visions must be a model.

1708. The dream to the grand must be a model.

Moral

1709. Moral values continuously increase our credibility.

1710. Moral values help us a lot in maintaining effective co operations.

1711. Moral values make us more credible.

1712. Moral values help us a lot to achieve effective co operations.

1713. Moral values create most of the times great masterpieces.

1714. Unfortunately, in 2010, there still are irresponsible behaviors of many people that negatively affect other people more or less. It is necessary and mandatory that all of these illegal behaviors are punished with tickets corresponding to their gravity and that they pay the damages and moral or psychical sufferings created in order to prevent repeating other irresponsible behaviors.

1715. Good morale greatly increases our ability to have self-control in any situation.

1716. Good morale greatly increases our chances of not getting in the situation of despair.

1717. If we do not have a good morale, we can shape it ourselves.

1718. As we have more experience, the more chances we have to achieve an optimal morale.

1719. Good morale helps us very much to achieve effective co operations.

1720. Good morale helps us very much in achieving records.

1721. Good morale helps us a lot to us achieve personal goals.

1722. Good morale helps us greatly to achieve a greater efficiency.

1723. Good morale needs to be kept constant, every day, for as long as we live.

1724. An optimal morale increases our chances of not reaching panic situations.

1725. An optimal morale can be formed through a proper diet, education, intellectual exercises, perseverance, will, physical exercises, etc.

1726. An optimal morale increases our chances of not reaching the situations of despair.

1727. Self education helps us form an optimal morale.

1728. An optimal morale helps us achieve an efficient development.

1729. Physical beauty without moral beauty sometimes destroys itself.

1730. A journalist who knowingly, for some reward, misinforms private citizens has no moral right to be a journalist, but also because legally his facts are crimes.

1731. There are men who appreciate more the moral beauty than the physical beauty of a woman.

1732. The moral beauty of a woman complements her natural beauty and makes her more attractive.

1733. Natural beauty without a moral one sometimes self-destroys.

1734. A judge who made a single injustice, has no moral right to judge. What to say to those who do daily tens of deeds of injustice, or annually thousands of deeds of injustice?

Mistakes

1735. Learning from other people's mistakes helps us achieve more favorable situations.

1736. Preventing mistakes helps us achieve much good luck.

1737. Learning from the others' mistakes helps us achieve more efficient co operations.

1738. Learning from other people's mistakes helps us achieve more performances.

1739. Preventing mistakes helps us achieve more pleasant surprises.

1740. Preventing mistakes helps us achieve more favorable chances.

1741. Learning from the others' mistakes helps us achieve more pleasant surprises.

1742. Learning from other people's mistakes helps us achieve more personal goals.

1743. Learning from our mistakes helps us achieve more efficient co operations.

1744. Learning from the others' mistakes helps us achieve much good luck.

1745. Learning from other people's mistakes helps us achieve more true friendships.

1746. Learning from our mistakes helps us achieve more favorable chances.

1747. Learning from other people's mistakes helps us achieve more successes.

1748. Learning from the others' mistakes helps us achieve more records.

1749. Learning from the others' mistakes helps us achieve more successes.

1750. Learning from the others' mistakes helps us achieve more performances.

1751. Learning from the others' mistakes helps us achieve more favorable chances.

Motivate

1752. In order to pursue and transform positive objectives into reality it is necessary to form and develop the ability to know how to motivate people.

1753. Obtaining as many and greatest successes as we can, can be achieved through the formation, development and maintenance of the ability to motivate people.

1754. Positive experience can be achieved also through the contribution of the formation, development and maintenance of the ability to efficiently motivate people.

1755. By listening very carefully to what people who have had successes say and by taking useful ideas from them we can form, develop, maintain and use the ideas of that help us motivate ourselves.

1756. We can contribute to achieving our happiness also through the contribution of the formation, development, maintenance and usage of the ability to motivate ourselves.

1757. Obstacles that stop us from achieving our personal goals can be overcome also through the contribution of the formation, development, maintenance and usage of ideas that motivate others.

1758. We can prevent some mistakes also through the formation of the formation, development, maintenance and usage of the ability to motivate ourselves.

1759. People with human social behaviors have a great ability to motivate people.

1760. People who have had successes mostly have known how to motivate people.

1761. People who want to obtain success must form and develop the ability to motivate people.

1762. Persons who have not succeeded in forming a happy marriage up to a certain date, in order to succeed they need to develop the ability of knowing how to motivate.

1763. People who do not have hopes, in order to create hopes for the future, need to connect with people who know how to motivate people.

1764. Efficient people in positive actions must be motivated.

1765. Those who know how to take quality decisions form and develop the ability to motivate people.

1766. In order to change your desire of changing it is really necessary to form, develop, maintain and use the ability to efficiently motivate people.

1767. By listening very carefully to what people who have had successes say and by taking from them the ideas that are useful to us we can form, develop, maintain and use the ideas that help us motivate ourselves.

1768. A conscious man, through his consciousness, motivates other people as well.

1769. Those who live life passionately also have the ability to motivate people.

1770. The ability to anticipate people's needs helps us motivate people in different actions.

1771. Those who willingly express their positive experience have of greater ability to achieve a motivated life.

1772. People who know how to motivate other people have more chances to achieve a mature love.

1773. People who know how to motivate other people have a greater ability to prevent more possible mistakes.

1774. People who know how to motivate other people have more and greater chances to meet more and greater favorable situations.

Optimism

1775. Optimism is one of the weapons that obtain successes.

1776. Success creates optimism.

1777. Successes create optimism.

1778. Optimism is a factor of many successes.

1779. Many times optimism is contagious.

1780. Optimism help us a lot to us achieve a more beautiful life.

1781. Failures should never defeat our optimism.

1782. Hopes are creators of optimism.

1783. Optimism helps us achieve performances.

1784. Optimism helps us get rid of stress.

1785. Optimism prevents us from reaching the state of despair.

1786. Optimism helps us increase our chances of achieving a more beautiful live.

1787. A good state of health contributes a lot to maintaining our optimism.

1788. Optimism increases our chances very much to achieve true friendships.

1789. A nervous state reduces our optimism.

1790. Optimism helps us get through life's difficulties a lot easier.

1791. Self delusion reduces our optimism.

1792. Discipline maintains optimism.

1793. Optimism leads us towards successes.

1794. Optimism helps us a lot and increases our chances to achieve a happy marriage.

1795. An optimistic man through his optimism motivates people.

1796. Optimism is an advantage in front of hardship.

1797. Optimism increases the chances of achieving more efficient co-developments.

1798. Optimism is the state that helps us obtain more and greater successes.

1799. Optimism increases are possibilities of achieving a mature love.

1800. An optimistic man has succeeded in building the achievements on his optimism.

1801. The state of restlessness reduces a lot our optimism.

1802. The state of fatigue reduces a lot our optimism.

1803. Optimism helps us a lot to increase our chances and prevent stress.

1804. Pessimism can be removed and replaced with optimism also through the contribution of the formation, development, maintenance and usage of positive thinking.

1805. Those who have not succeeded to achieve a happy marriage up to a certain date need to form and develop the ability of forming and developing strategies of formation, development and maintenance of optimism.

1806. Pessimism can be removed and replaced with optimism also through the contribution of the formation, development, maintenance and usage of the long term thinking.

1807. Pessimism can be removed and replaced with optimism also through the contribution of the formation, development, maintenance and usage of the ability to achieve the necessary efficient co operations.

1808. Pessimism can be removed and replaced with optimism also through the contribution of the formation, development, maintenance and usage of creative thinking.

1809. Pessimism must be replaced with optimism in any situation.

1810. We can eliminate pessimism and replace it with optimism also through the contribution of the formation, development, maintenance and usage of optimistic ideas.

1811. Desperation can be eliminated also through the contribution of the formation, development, maintenance and usage of optimism.

1812. Pessimism can be eliminated and replaced with optimism also through the contribution of the formation, development, maintenance and usage of efficient co operations.

1813. In order to pursue and transform our personal goals into reality we need to form, develop, maintain and use optimism.

1814. Pessimism can be removed and replaced with optimism also through the contribution of the formation, development, maintenance and usage of constructive thinking.

1815. Pessimism can be removed and replaced with optimism also through the contribution of the formation, development, maintenance and usage of the ability to form and use positive behaviors.

1816. Pessimism can be eliminated and replaced with optimism also through the contribution of the formation, development, maintenance and usage of positive thinking.

1817. In order to pursue and transform positive objectives into reality it is necessary to form and develop the ability to form and maintain optimism.

1818. Rather than lamenting that we do not have successes it is better to form, develop and support optimism.

1819. Optimism brings people together.

1820. Optimism creates enthusiasm.

1821. Optimism must be taken as a model.

1822. Optimism must replace pessimism.

1823. Optimism is also created by optimistic thinking.

1824. Optimism is also created by positive thinking.

1825. Pessimism can be removed and replaced with optimism also through the contribution of the formation, development, maintenance and usage of cheerful behavior.

1826. Optimism helps us become decisive.

1827. Optimism helps us become docile.

1828. A great capacity of achieving what was proposed helps us maintain our optimism.

1829. Pessimism can be removed and replaced with optimism also through the contribution

of the formation, development, maintenance and usage of behavior of being interested in any useful information.

1830. Pessimism can be removed and replaced with optimism also through the contribution of the formation, development, maintenance and usage of sportive behavior.

1831. Optimism helps us become firm.

1832. Pessimism can be removed and replaced with optimism also through the contribution of the formation, development, maintenance and usage of spiritual behavior.

1833. Optimism helps us become reserved.

1834. Optimism helps us become harmless.

1835. Pessimism can be removed and replaced with optimism also through the contribution of the formation, development, maintenance and usage of persistent behavior.

1836. A great capacity of maintaining relationships with people helps us maintain our optimism.

1837. Pessimism can be removed and replaced with optimism also through the contribution

of the formation, development, maintenance and usage of harmless behavior.

1838. The desire to be grand helps us maintain our optimism.

1839. Pessimism can be removed and replaced with optimism also through the contribution of the formation, development, maintenance and usage of understanding behavior.

1840. A great capacity of assuming the necessary risks for success helps us maintain our optimism.

1841. Pessimism can be removed and replaced with optimism also through the contribution of the formation, development, maintenance and usage of sensible behavior.

1842. Pessimism can be removed and replaced with optimism also through the contribution of the formation, development, maintenance and usage of tenacious behavior.

1843. Pessimism can be removed and replaced with optimism also through the contribution of the formation, development, maintenance and usage of astute behavior.

1844. Pessimism can be removed and replaced with optimism also through the contribution of the formation, development, maintenance and usage of humane behavior.

1845. Optimism helps us become mannered.

1846. A great capacity of rapid instruction helps us maintain our optimism.

1847. Pessimism can be removed and replaced with optimism also through the contribution of the formation, development, maintenance and usage of abstract behavior.

1848. Optimism helps us become patient.

1849. A great capacity of using each failure to achieve successes helps us maintain our optimism.

1850. A great capacity of establishing great personal goals helps us maintain our optimism.

1851. Pessimism can be removed and replaced with optimism also through the contribution of the formation, development, maintenance and usage of friendly behavior.

1852. Pessimism can be removed and replaced with optimism also through the contribution of the formation, development, maintenance and usage of the loyal behavior.

1853. A great capacity of being tolerant with people helps us maintain our optimism.

1854. A great capacity of gathering our energies helps us maintain our optimism.

1855. A great capacity of being convincing helps us maintain our optimism.

1856. Pessimism can be removed and replaced with optimism also through the contribution of the formation, development, maintenance and usage of voluble behavior.

1857. A great capacity of not letting others lead one's life helps us maintain our optimism.

1858. Pessimism can be removed and replaced with optimism also through the contribution of the formation, development, maintenance and usage of optimistic behavior.

1859. Pessimism can be removed and replaced with optimism also through the contribution of the formation, development, maintenance and usage of funny behavior.

1860. A great capacity of continuously overcoming boundaries helps us maintain our optimism.

1861. Pessimism can be removed and replaced with optimism also through the contribution of the formation, development, maintenance and usage of confident behavior.

1862. Pessimism can be removed and replaced with optimism also through the contribution of the formation, development, maintenance and usage of logical behavior.

1863. A great capacity of using available ideas helps us maintain our optimism.

1864. Pessimism can be removed and replaced with optimism also through the contribution of the formation, development, maintenance and usage of realistic behavior.

1865. Pessimism can be removed and replaced with optimism also through the contribution of the formation, development, maintenance and usage of peaceful behavior.

1866. Pessimism can be removed and replaced with optimism also through the contribution of the formation, development, maintenance and usage of content behavior.

1867. A great capacity of applying strategies of thinking big style helps us maintain our optimism.

1868. Pessimism can be removed and replaced with optimism also through the contribution of the formation, development, maintenance and usage of fighting behavior.

1869. Pessimism can be removed and replaced with optimism also through the contribution of the formation, development, maintenance and usage of cautious behavior.

1870. Optimism helps us become convincing.

1871. Optimism helps us become popular.

1872. Optimism helps us become optimistic.

1873. Pessimism can be removed and replaced with optimism also through the contribution of the formation, development, maintenance and usage of trained behavior.

1874. Pessimism can be removed and replaced with optimism also through the contribution of the formation, development, maintenance and usage of continuous self motivating behavior.

1875. A great capacity of encouraging people helps us maintain our optimism.

1876. Optimism helps us become tenacious.

1877. Optimism helps us become rigorous.

1878. A great capacity of being popular helps us maintain our optimism.

1879. Pessimism can be removed and replaced with optimism also through the contribution of the formation, development, maintenance and usage of decent behavior.

1880. Pessimism can be removed and replaced with optimism also through the contribution of the formation, development, maintenance and usage of firm behavior.

1881. Pessimism can be removed and replaced with optimism also through the contribution of the formation, development, maintenance and usage of ingenious behavior.

1882. Pessimism can be removed and replaced with optimism also through the contribution of the formation, development, maintenance and usage of inventive behavior.

1883. A great capacity of understanding others helps us maintain our optimism.

1884. Optimism helps us become joyful.

1885. Pessimism can be removed and replaced with optimism also through the contribution of the formation, development, maintenance and usage of ruling behavior.

1886. Pessimism can be removed and replaced with optimism also through the contribution of the formation, development, maintenance and usage of unpretentious behavior.

1887. A great capacity of more efficiently using financial means helps us maintain our optimism.

1888. A great capacity of increasing creativity helps us maintain our optimism.

1889. Optimism helps us become positive.

1890. Pessimism can be removed and replaced with optimism also through the contribution of the formation, development, maintenance and usage of mannered behavior.

1891. A great capacity of using each personal mistake to achieve successes helps us maintain our optimism.

1892. A great capacity of being friendly helps us maintain our optimism.

1893. A great capacity of drawing attention helps us maintain our optimism.

1894. Pessimism can be removed and replaced with optimism also through the contribution of the formation, development, maintenance and usage of reasonable behavior.

1895. A great capacity of being honest with oneself helps us maintain our optimism.

1896. Pessimism can be removed and replaced with optimism also through the contribution of the formation, development, maintenance and usage of pleasant behavior.

1897. Optimism helps us become analytic.

1898. A great capacity of maintaining self confidence helps us maintain our optimism.

1899. Pessimism can be removed and replaced with optimism also through the contribution

of the formation, development, maintenance and usage of perfectionist behavior.

1900. A great capacity of having an even more energetic life helps us maintain our optimism.

1901. A great capacity of working hard helps us maintain our optimism.

1902. Optimism helps us become expansive.

1903. Pessimism can be removed and replaced with optimism also through the contribution of the formation, development, maintenance and usage of self-controlled behavior.

1904. Pessimism can be removed and replaced with optimism also through the contribution of the formation, development, maintenance and usage of charming behavior.

1905. Pessimism can be removed and replaced with optimism also through the contribution of the formation, development, maintenance and usage of daring behavior.

1906. A great capacity of using available resources helps us maintain our optimism.

1907. Optimism helps us become balanced.

1908. Pessimism can be removed and replaced with optimism also through the contribution of the formation, development, maintenance and usage of sensitive behavior.

1909. Pessimism can be removed and replaced with optimism also through the contribution of the formation, development, maintenance and usage of systematic behavior.

1910. A great capacity of managing life helps us maintain our optimism.

1911. Optimism helps us become active.

1912. Optimism helps us become sincere.

1913. Optimism helps us become energetic.

1914. Optimism helps us become sturdy.

1915. Pessimism can be removed and replaced with optimism also through the contribution of the formation, development, maintenance and usage of continuous self economizing behavior.

1916. Pessimism can be removed and replaced with optimism also through the contribution of the formation, development, maintenance and usage of respectful behavior.

1917. Pessimism can be removed and replaced with optimism also through the contribution of the formation, development, maintenance and usage of diplomatic behavior.

1918. Optimism helps us become consequent.

1919. Pessimism can be removed and replaced with optimism also through the contribution of the formation, development, maintenance and usage of efficient behavior.

1920. Pessimism can be removed and replaced with optimism also through the contribution of the formation, development, maintenance and usage of attachable behavior.

1921. Optimism helps us become sure of ourselves.

Optimistic

1922. When we are depressed it is necessary to get in contact with optimistic people and to do things which bring us success, achievements and hopes.

1923. It is never too late to become optimistic again.

1924. Relationships with optimistic people make us much more optimistic.

1925. Through co operation we can become more optimistic a lot sooner.

1926. It is always necessary to be surrounded by optimistic people.

1927. Mutual love makes us much more optimistic.

1928. When our moral is down, we need to study books on positive thinking, to begin relationships with optimistic people.

1929. Hopes always make us more optimistic.

1930. Optimistic people are optimistic because they have hope.

1931. As we have more hopes we are much more optimistic.

1932. Optimistic people have achieved the great accomplishments of mankind.

1933. Our objectives make us become optimistic or more optimistic.

1934. If we are pessimistic it is possible to have more failures than if we would be optimistic.

1935. Positive thinking makes us much more optimistic.

1936. An optimistic man most of the times achieves himself in life.

1937. An optimistic man many times has many hopes.

1938. Usually, those who are optimistic are more active.

1939. An optimistic man has more and greater chances to harmoniously develop his personality.

1940. Experience makes us more confident in ourselves and more optimistic.

1941. People who have success are mostly more optimistic than the others.

1942. The majority of people who have successes are optimistic.

1943. An optimistic man through his optimism motivates people.

1944. Those who have no hopes, in order to create their hopes in the future, need to connect with people who are optimistic.

1945. An optimistic man more easily and quickly achieves true friendships.

1946. Most of the times an optimistic man is also a sincere man.

1947. A pessimistic man has fewer and smaller achievements than the optimistic one.

1948. An efficient man is more optimistic than an inefficient man.

1949. An optimistic man always thinks a lot about the future.

1950. An optimistic man many times has a great desire to succeed in life.

1951. An optimistic man has succeeded in building the achievements on his optimism.

1952. Hopes can be created through the contribution of the formation, development, maintenance and usage of optimistic ideas.

1953. Despair can be eliminated also through the contribution of the formation, development, maintenance and usage of optimistic ideas.

1954. In order to prevent the failure of our personal goals it is necessary to form, develop, maintain and use only optimistic ideas.

1955. The desire to make others happy can be really achieved also through the contribution of the formation, development, maintenance and achievement of optimistic ideas.

1956. We can replace wrong ideas with correct ideas also through the contribution of the formation, development, maintenance and usage of an optimistic life conception.

1957. Stress can be prevented also through the contribution of the formation, development, maintenance and usage of optimistic behaviors.

1958. Those without hopes for the future need to become friends with those who are optimistic.

1959. People with no hopes for the future need to connect with those who have become optimistic.

1960. Emancipation from self imposed restrictions can be made through the formation, development and maintenance of optimistic thinking.

1961. Forming wrong ideas can be prevented also through the formation, development, maintenance and usage of optimistic ideas.

1962. Preventing the formation of doubts can also be achieved through the formation, development, maintenance and usage of optimistic thinking.

1963. In order to stand up once again, be it for the first time, for the second time, for the who knows what time, it is necessary to form, develop, maintain and use optimistic thinking.

1964. Finding the meaning of our lives can be achieved also through the contribution of the formation, development, maintenance and usage of an optimistic conception of life.

1965. Hopes can be created also through the contribution of the formation, development, maintenance and usage of an optimistic conception of life.

1966. In order to change the desire of changing into reality it is necessary to form, develop, maintain and use optimistic thinking.

1967. We can become stronger and we cannot let ourselves be influenced by the world also through the contribution of the formation, development, maintenance and usage of an optimistic live conception.

1968. Abilities can be formed, developed, maintained and used also through the contribution of formation, development, maintenance and usage of optimistic behaviors.

1969. Desperation can be overcome also through the contribution of the formation, development, maintenance and usage of an optimistic conception of life.

1970. We can form, develop, maintain and use an open mind also through the contribution of the formation, development, maintenance and usage of optimistic thinking.

1971. The force of our ideas can be enhanced also through the contribution of the formation, development, maintenance and usage of an optimistic conception of life.

1972. The desire to make others happy can be achieved through the contribution of the formation, development, maintenance and achievement of optimistic thinking.

1973. The desire to make udders happy can be achieved through the contribution of the formation, development, maintenance and achievement of optimistic ideas.

1974. We can replace wrong ideas with correct ideas also through the contribution of the formation, development, maintenance and usage of an optimistic conception of life.

1975. Stressing can be prevented also through the contribution of the formation, development, maintenance and usage of optimistic behaviors.

1976. We can broaden our horizon even more through the contribution of the formation, development, maintenance and usage of optimistic conception.

1977. Forming the wrong ideas about what is happening to us can be prevented also through the formation, development, maintenance and usage of an optimistic conception of life.

1978. Those who do not think enough need to form, develop, maintain and use an optimistic conception of life.

1979. In achieving successes a contribution is brought by the formation, development, maintenance and usage of optimistic behaviors.

1980. We can eliminate pessimism and replace it with optimism also through the contribution of the formation, development, maintenance and usage of optimistic ideas.

1981. In order to escape poverty it is necessary to form, develop, maintain and use optimistic thinking.

1982. Finding the meaning of our lives can be achieved also through the contribution of the formation, development, maintenance and usage of optimistic thinking.

1983. We can broaden our horizon even more through the contribution of the formation, development, maintenance and usage of an optimistic conception of life.

1984. Desperation can be eliminated also through the contribution of the formation, development, maintenance and usage of an optimistic behavior.

1985. The solutions to the problems we have for the problems we want to solve can be found also through the contribution of the formation, development, maintenance and usage of optimistic thinking.

1986. Hopes can be created also through the contribution of the formation, development, maintenance and usage of optimistic ideas.

1987. In order to prevent not achieving our personal goals it is necessary to form, develop, maintain and use only optimistic ideas.

1988. In order to pursue and transform our personal goals into reality we need to form, develop, maintain and use the ability to be optimistic.

1989. Finding the meaning of our life can be achieved also through using optimistic ideas.

1990. Doubts can be prevented through the formation, development, maintenance and usage of optimistic thinking.

1991. Preventing wrong ideas is achieved through the analysis of optimistic thinking.

1992. Problems can be solved only through optimistic thinking.

1993. Despair can be eliminated through the formation, development, maintenance and usage of optimistic life conceptions.

1994. Stress can be prevented through the development, maintenance and usage of optimistic behaviors.

1995. Efficient ideas can be developed through the formation, maintenance and usage of optimistic thinking.

1996. Optimistic women have more chances to become more efficient.

1997. Pessimism can be removed through the contribution of the formation, development, maintenance and usage of optimistic behaviors.

1998. Optimistic thinking helps us socialize.

1999. Despair can be eliminated through optimistic thinking.

2000. Emancipation from restrictions can be made through the formation, development and maintenance of optimistic thinking.

2001. Forming wrong ideas can be prevented through the contribution of the formation, development, maintenance and usage of optimistic ideas.

2002. Preventing the formation of doubts can be achieved also through the formation, development, maintenance and usage of optimistic thinking.

2003. In order to rise up once again for the first time, for the second time, for the who knows what time, it is necessary to form, develop, maintain and use optimistic thinking.

2004. Finding the meaning of our lives can be achieved also through the contribution of the formation, development, maintenance and usage of an optimistic life conception.

2005. Hopes can be created also through the contribution of the formation, development, maintenance and usage of an optimistic life conception.

2006. Doubts can be eliminated through the formation, development, maintenance and usage of an optimistic life conception.

2007. A great capacity of using attitudes helps us become more optimistic.

Positive

2008. Positive ideas should be always taken into account.

2009. Positive ideas are the engines of progress.

2010. Positive ideas should be storaged in idea banks.

2011. Positive actions surely take us to larger or smaller successes, even if we realize them with bigger or smaller efforts.

2012. Behavior for luxury can be prevented by positive thinking.

2013. Selflessness is a model of positive behavior that is necessary to appreciate.

2014. Positive facts have multiple positive effects.

2015. Positive facts should be valued.

2016. Positive actions should be taken as models.

2017. Positive actions prevent many negative actions.

2018. Positive actions should be appreciated.

2019. Supporting positive action is a necessity.

2020. Popularization of positive actions is a necessity.

2021. While making positive facts we cannot make negative facts.

2022. While we think of positive facts we can no longer think of negative facts.

2023. Positive ideas always have to be cherished.

2024. When the future seems desperate it is necessary to study books on positive thinking.

2025. We can prevent bitterness by thinking positively.

2026. Positive behaviors lead us to happiness.

2027. The aid given at the necessary time often has incredible positive effects.

2028. Anger can be prevented by thinking positive.

2029. Positive thinking guides us to success.

2030. Through a positive thinking we can overcome our desires.

2031. Through a positive thinking we can prevent many, many troubles.

2032. Through positive actions we can prevent many failures.

2033. We can prevent sorrows through a positive thinking.

2034. By acting continuously and effectively to achieve positive goals we will surely achieve them.

2035. Many problems can be avoided by thinking positive.

2036. Positive tips are a resource to our happiness.

2037. Some positive special facts create heroes.

2038. The more idols we have the more necessary it is that all our behaviors be positive.

2039. Successes are also effects of positive thinking.

2040. Objectivity is essential to positive action.

2041. Positive thinking prevents much harm.

2042. By having a positive thinking we can prevent many mistakes.

2043. Young people of the world's states, unfortunately, do not use their capacities and qualities, skills, abilities, attitudes, knowledge, and the enormous energy that they have, their enthusiasm and optimism, which are positive things, the desire of affirmation and of making achievements in order to participate in the activity of communal, municipal, departmental, regional councils of counties, of parliaments, of governments, etc..

2044. Those who will consider positive pieces of advice will have more chances to achieve more performances.

2045. Many problems can be avoided if we have a positive thinking.

2046. Failures in life can be many times prevented also through a positive thought.

2047. We can prevent more failures if we analyze our actions, their positive and negative effects, so that we and others achieve and avoid actions with negative, risky, illegal effects.

2048. The more positive and humane deeds we accomplish, the more we increase our chances of being happy.

2049. Positive thinking helps us create only positive ideas, which, in turn, help us achieve only positive deeds.

2050. Not recognizing a man's positive facts damages him.

2051. Humor has positive effects on health.

2052. Positive facts need to be appreciated.

2053. Happiness has positive effects on health.

2054. In life, it is necessary to allow ourselves to be influenced only by positive influences, and when facing potential negative influences we must be immune.

2055. We must be receptive to any positive ideas.

2056. Those who are very receptive to all positive ideas, as opposed to those who are not, are able to achieve more successes in life.

2057. Positive ideas need to be sustained, continuously promoted and applied with the greatest efficiency.

2058. For the sake of ourselves and of others, of human society, it is necessary and mandatory to appreciate and respect positive thinking.

2059. For our sake and that of others, of human society, it is necessary and required to appreciate, promote and apply positive ideas.

2060. For our sake and that of others, of human society, it is necessary and required to appreciate, promote and apply positive programs and projects.

2061. For our sake and that of others, of human society, it is necessary to appreciate, reward and promote positive actions.

2062. Through a positive thinking we can overcome envy.

2063. Positive ideas translated into positive actions make us become happy.

2064. Positive and effective ideas definitely lead us in achieving our objectives.

2065. Those who have an iron will and perseverance have very high chances to achieve their positive and realistic goals.

2066. A positive, effective way of life makes our life happy.

2067. While entering into relationships with other people it is good to take from them as much positive experience and knowledge as we can because they help us achieve the happiness that we all want for ourselves.

2068. The continuous search for positive and useful knowledge should be a primary objective of ours for as long as we live.

2069. Only positive and useful knowledge to us can help us continue to achieve positive realistic goals.

2070. Our inner potential can be greatly increased on a continuous basis by: 1) the study of more books, 2) by browsing the Internet, 3) by taking, from people who have had great success, their positive experience and ideas etc..

2071. The positive knowledge is that which we accumulate form our way of life.

2072. As we accumulate more positive knowledge required to achieve our objectives the more we become more able to achieve then.

2073. Ideas come fast and we forget them even faster. Ideas come out continuously, without us making any effort. Ideas that we seek, that we want to find we sometimes find them easily, other times very difficult and sometimes we can not fiind anything without looking better.

2074. Our ability to create ideas is a mine which can increase the value and on a continuous basis, without great efforts.

2075. Our ability to create ideas can continuously increase for as long as we live, thus increasing its value on a continuous basis. Our ability to create ideas affects us enormously in our achievement and maintenance of our happiness every day in every situation.

2076. The desire to obtain performance is necessary and must be positive for performance because it is good for some and unfortunately negative for others.

2077. Forming, developing and rewarding positive performance in children makes us not have performers in negative performance, namely criminals.

2078. The desire to achieve positive performance helps us meet our needs.

2079. Involvement in positive activities helps us become more sociable.

2080. Single people can get rid of loneliness when involved in positive activities.

2081. It is required to get rid of loneliness and to have a positive thinking.

2082. It is required to get rid of loneliness and to have a positive thought.

2083. Involvement in positive activities is a necessity for all of us.

2084. Positive thinking helps us form an active and positive lifestyle.

2085. We can remove the feeling of loneliness through our involvement in positive activities as much as possible.

2086. Through will and perseverance we can change our passive lifestyle into an active positive one.

2087. Positive ideas have always been supported.

2088. Positive ideas should be promoted as much as possible.

2089. Positive ideas are the only ideas that help us and contribute to the achievement of personal goals.

2090. Positive ideas help us achieve successes.

2091. Positive ideas should be supported to take the place of negative ideas.

2092. We must create the conditions so that sociable people achieve their objectives as soon as their objectives have positive effects on people.

2093. Positive principles help us achieve personal goals.

2094. Positive principles help us be more appreciated.

2095. The respect of the wife towards the husband is achieved through a positive behavior of her husband towards her and the other members of his family.

2096. Positive ideas should always be supported.

2097. Developing positive thinking leads to the creation of more positive ideas.

2098. Positive thinking prevents many negative facts.

2099. Positive thinking helps us become happy.

2100. Positive thinking is a part of wisdom.

2101. Developing positive thinking creates more wealth.

2102. Correct relations of friendship make us happy and have positive effects on our health.

2103. Life has positive effects on health.

2104. We must make changes only when specifically requested by the actual situation and when they have positive effects greater than the costs and negative effects.

2105. People who have a positive attitude are preferred by employers. A positive attitude is a quality and a key to obtaining the work we desire and to keep us as an employee. If you do not have a positive attitude, it is no problem, you can learn if you want, it can be learned easily. Good luck! I'm with you.

2106. Positive facts increase our credibility.

2107. The more positive facts we achieve the more credibility we have in the face of people.

2108. If you want credibility respect your commitments. Let your words become facts. Achieve as many positive facts as you can. Be humane. Help people when you can. Be close to people in a sincere way. Be selfless always when necessary.

2109. Positive global human solidarity helps us achieve much more efficient positive global co operations.

2110. A positive conception of life helps us and increases our chances of a mature true love.

2111. Those who have high preferences for uncontrollable positive activism have a high potential of achieving a happy life.

2112. Those who have high preferences for uncontrollable positive activism have the potential and big chances to achieve great outstanding performances.

2113. Those who have wise friends can learn many positive efficient behaviors.

2114. Those who have co operations with wise men can learn a lot from their efficient positive behaviors.

2115. It is always necessary to adapt to efficient positive changes in society.

2116. Those who adapt to efficient positive changes in society will be successful.

2117. Those who adapt to efficient positive changes in society will achieve their personal goals and projects.

2118. Those who adapt to efficient positive changes in society will have much more chances to meet more favorable situations.

2119. New ideas must not only be new but also positive and better.

2120. The activity of producing positive ideas is the most efficient human activity.

2121. Our activity of producing positive ideas helps us the most to continuously increase our efficiency.

2122. Positive models help us achieve a happy marriage.

2123. Positive models help us achieve our personal goals.

2124. Positive models help us achieve successes.

2125. Positive models help us have more chances of meeting more favorable situations.

2126. Positive ideas are the engines of progress in all areas of activity.

2127. Positive ideas are the engines of achievement of personal goals.

2128. Positive ideas motivate people to act.

2129. Personal values provoke people to positive actions.

2130. There are situations which influence our life in a positive way even more than years or dozens of years.

2131. Positive global human solidarity helps us achieve many positive, human, global co operations.

2132. A positive conception of life helps us and increases our chances to become more credible.

2133. Those with high preferences for unstoppable positive activism become more credible.

2134. Those with high preferences for unstoppable positive activism become more efficient.

2135. A positive efficient human communication contributes a lot to achieving many true friendships.

2136. Without positive ideas no progress in any area of activity can be achieved.

2137. Dates, the institutions of states, the local communities need to support, stimulate, and reward positive human actions, that are good for people, that occupy their time in a positive way and for their own good.

2138. In life, we must not behave like x or y says, but according to the way we think it is best, positive, correct, legal and human.

2139. Achieving many short term personal goals positively influence some or all long term personal goals.

2140. The successes we have obtained have created a special positive experience.

2141. Our achieved successes are sources of positive models for present and future behaviors for all of us.

2142. Successes, the stages to achieving successes are very valuable treasures of positive experience.

Qualities

2143. Each of us surely has a higher or lower number of qualities. It is for our own good and for our happiness to discover them and then to use them as much as we can in order to make us happy.

2144. Each of us surely has a higher or lower number of qualities. It is for our own good and for our happiness to discover them and then to use them as much as we can in order to make us happy.

2145. Each of us has a bigger or smaller number of qualities.

2146. It is never too late to self-develop certain qualities.

2147. It is necessary at all times to develop our human qualities.

2148. Those that have more qualities have more opportunities to make themselves happy.

2149. Our qualities make a lot of us very happy.

2150. Human qualities contribute the most to human success.

2151. Young people of the world's states, unfortunately, do not use their capacities and qualities, skills, abilities, attitudes, knowledge, and the enormous energy that they have, their enthusiasm and optimism, which are positive things, the desire of affirmation and of making achievements in order to participate in the activity of communal, municipal, departmental, regional councils of counties, of parliaments, of governments, etc..

2152. Human qualities contribute the most to human successes.

2153. Human qualities make a lot of people happy.

2154. Persons with many qualities are respected.

2155. Persons with many qualities are valued.

2156. Persons with many qualities are more likely to achieve more successes than those who have fewer skills.

2157. Persons with many qualities have very big chances to achieve successes.

2158. A man with qualities is appreciated.

2159. The more qualities we have, the more and greater opportunities we have to achieve more successes.

2160. The fact that we do not have certain assets, accomplishments, etc. during certain periods of our life must not fret, consume, frustrate, make us unhappy, but it is necessary to enjoy what we have, what we have achieved, the projects that we have to achieve, the qualities, the skills that we have, etc.

2161. I esteem women very much, appreciate and respect them very much for what they are, for the special qualities that they have.

2162. It is essential that much more women set as goals the prevention of divorce, of unhappy marriages and that they work to achieve them, because fortunately they will most certainly succeed because many have the qualities and capabilities required to do this.

2163. By developing their inner beauty, the qualities, skills, abilities and feelings that make them happy, women can create more joy and satisfactions.

2164. Knowing yourself is very necessary and very useful to us in order to achieve a happy marriage, to maintain it, to make friends and to maintain them, to use cover our qualities and flaws, etc.

2165. Men need to appreciate, respect all the qualities of women no matter what the situation is, even in this situation when these have more qualities than them.

2166. The husband who has a wife with more qualities than he does needs to be proud of her, to respect her, appreciate and support her, help her use her qualities for her sake, their children's sake and her husband's sake.

2167. The life of each of us is influenced by us once, that is the by our internal factors, which are very large in number, among which we can remember: 1) our health, 2) our values, 3) our objectives, 4) our qualities 5) our thinking, 6) if we think long term or short-term, or joined, completed, 7) our ability, 8) our gender, 9) our age, etc.

2168. There are certain situations in marriage when women have more and more qualities and greater achievements than men. In these circumstances the man should not feel inferior, complexed, frustated, moody, disturbed by the situation, etc.. but instead he should see the good side of the situation, to enjoy a lot of the qualities and achievements of his wife, to be proud of her, to stimulate, appreciate and respect her more and assist her in achieving her objectives, to help her when she need his help and he can give it to her.

2169. If I had a wife with many qualities, with many achievements, with more quality than me, with more and bigger achievements than me, I would enjoy it very much, I would be very happy, happy of her outstanding achievements, qualities, I would not feel complexed by her achievements, I would not feel disturbed, frustated, not envious, but I would want much more results and I would support her as I could to achieve her special objectives.

2170. Persons with many qualities are especially dear.

2171. Human qualities make many families happy.

2172. Each of us is necessary to determine what qualities we need in order to achieve the objectives we have set. If we do not have certain qualities, it is necessary to analyze and determine if we can shape and develop them. If we can shape and then develop them it is necessary then to form and develop them.

2173. In order to achieve personal goals with greater opportunities it is necessary to develop the qualities needed to achieve these goals.

2174. Many people of the planet's people which consider themselves unhappy, have the qualities necessary to start, step by step, in a thoughtful way to achieve their own happiness through setting their own personal goal to achieve their own happiness for as long as they live.

2175. Each of us with the help of the qualities that we have with that of those that we can shape and develop, of the various resources around the world, of the human experience and knowledge acquired in books, on the Internet, in publications, etc. we can be optimistic in our future in achieving a happy future. It is necessary to mobilize the will, qualities given to us with all our being to achieve the personal goal of making a happier future for us. Good luck to all. The ideas exposed by me can help very much, use them.

2176. Always in the creation and establishment of personal projects we must take into account our knowledge, qualities, abilities and our skills.

2177. If we establish personal projects for whose achievement we do not have the necessary knowledge, skills, qualities and abilities, we are very likely not to achieve them.

2178. People who are always concerned about the future also have creative qualities.

2179. It is always needed to develop capacities, skills, qualities and attitudes, but we need the development of our personality, it is necessary to have this as a personal objective.

2180. The more creative qualities we have and the greater capacity of creation, the more we can find and discover more favorable circumstances for ourselves.

2181. More of us would become happy and happier if they were more optimistic, if they knew their qualities, abilities, aptitudes and if they trusted themselves more.

2182. Each of us is necessary to discover all our qualities and to grow as much as possible to increase our chances to maintain a happy marriage.

2183. Some successes are due only to the qualities and exceptional efforts of people without the participation of any favorable circumstances.

2184. Even if we reached a desperate situation we can get rid of it easily mostly because it is written that we live better, not worse, because we have the qualities necessary for this but we should use them effectively.

2185. Continuously, every day it is necessary to have as a personal objective the training and development of those qualities that help us and contribute to the achievement of personal goals.

2186. As we have more capacities and qualities, the more chances we have to meet several favorable occasions.

2187. For as long as we live, continuously, day by day, it is necessary to have as a personal goal to form and develop as more creative qualities as we can.

2188. The more creative qualities we shape and develop, the more creative we become.

2189. The more qualities we shape and develop, the more opportunities we have to meet more favorable opportunities.

2190. The man who has a wife with several qualities should appreciate her more.

2191. A man must always appreciate the qualities of women.

2192. A leader does not like to be a leader with great success only if it has qualities and abilities to understand others as well.

2193. He who has an emotional intelligence consists of: 1) the ability to understand others, 2) the ability to help others when needed, with ideas, solutions, and even financial and material ones, a service to resolve the problem, etc.. 3) the ability to see things from the viewpoint of others; 4) the quality and ability to solve problems through relationships that you establish with others; 5) qualities; 6) human qualities; 7) has a good control in any situation; 8) has the ability to easily interact with people; 9) has the capacity and capability to maintain human relationships; 10) has high qualities and abilities to motivate people to mobilize them to work; 11) has the capacity and capability to push people to achieve objectives; 12) has the capacity and capability to keep us optimistic continuously and in any event, and even in very difficult ones; 13) has the ability to never give up under any circumstances even if it appears to others without a way out 14) has high qualities and the ability to trust people; 15) has high qualities and abilities that people have confidence in him, in his qualities; 16) has high qualities and the ability for people to come to the opinion of a request in solving many problems; 17) has high qualities and the ability to gather people around him; 18) has high qualities and the ability to trust himself ; 19) has instinct; 20) is reliable.

2194. If you want to reach parliament, you'll definitely get in: 1) if you know how to solve efficiently and timely issues for people, 2) if you promise to solve the problems of the people, 3) if you understand people and their problems; 4) if you develop continuously and daily your capacity and ability to understand others and their problems; 5) if you have the quality and ability to see things from the viewpoint of others, people who want to vote for you and need you to solve problems; 6) if you have humane qualities; 7) if you have the quality and ability to interact easily with people; 8) if you have a high quality and ability to maintain human relations; 9) if you have a quality and ability to motivate and mobilize people to action; 10) if you have a high quality and ability to motivate people to achieve objectives; 11) if you have the quality and ability to be optimistic continuously and in any circumstances, even in they are very difficult; 12) if you have the quality and ability never to give up in any situation even if you have not succeeded very often in solving a problem; 13) if you have a high quality and ability that people have confidence; 14) if you have a high quality and the ability to trust people; 15) if you have a great quality and ability for people to come to you to ask your opinion in solving many problems, 16) if you have a great quality and ability to gather people around, 17) the great quality and ability to trust yourself; 18) if you have instinct; 19) if you are reliable, fair, honest, 20) if you have a great quality and ability to be optimistic in any situation , no matter how difficult it is, etc. If you do not have them it does not matter. It is learned through learning and continuous exercise. So if you want to be a parliamentarian, learn and practice those listed and you are surely to succeed. Good luck.

2195. Qualities are the main factors of our prosperity.

2196. Appreciation of the other's qualities, of those who cooperate with us strengthen our cooperation.

2197. Appreciation of the qualities that we have unite us all.

2198. Those who are preoccupied with creating an optimal cooperation in a team have special qualities of achieving social relations.

2199. Those who are concerned with creating an optimal cooperation in a team have humanist qualities.

2200. Continuously, day by day, it is necessary to form and develop those qualities that help us contribute to the achievement of personal goals.

2201. We can create a beautiful life for ourselves if we have more qualities.

2202. If we have defects, we do not have the qualities necessary to do what we need to do and we have failures.

2203. Each of us is necessary to discover all the qualities and to grow as much as possible in order to increase our chances to achieve a true marriage.

2204. Some successes are due to the greatest extent to the qualities of people and less to favorable circumstances.

2205. For as long as we live we must seek to have relationships of friendship with special people, who have many successes, many qualities, many positive and effective behaviors in order to learn from them as much as possible. This rule, this principle helps us achieve much easier and more personal goals.

2206. In life we have more opportunities to meet favorable situations if we are friends with as many people who have had successes as possible, people which have qualities, skills, effective behaviors, creative qualities, which are well documented in the areas that concern us as well.

2207. Many of us have the qualities and skills necessary to grow and be educated properly, but unfortunately not all have the time needed and they make big, very big mistakes, which later are not good for anything that we did. Warning also to successful people who can prevent this mistake.

2208. Each of us needs to discover all his qualities and to grow as much as possible in order to increase our chances of achieving more and greater successes.

2209. Individual qualities help and contribute greatly to achieving successes.

2210. We must be happy with the qualities that we have and develop them continuously, day by day, and use them effectively so that we are effective.

2211. Each of us is necessary to discover the qualities and to grow them as much as possible in order to increase our chances of achieving our personal goals.

2212. The more qualities needed to achieve personal goals we have the more chances and opportunities we have to make fewer mistakes.

2213. Intellectual qualities are also an effect of education.

2214. Intellectual qualities can be developed continuously, day by day, for as long as we live.

2215. Intellectual qualities are more important to succeed in life.

2216. Intellectual qualities help us the most to achieve many personal goals.

2217. Intellectual qualities help us achieve effective co operations.

2218. Courage is also created by qualities that you have as a person.

2219. Moral qualities help us keep our happy marriage.

2220. Self-knowledge helps us form the qualities that we do not have but that we need.

2221. Children are suffering very high mental trauma when parents divorce. Dear parents, if you have children, before the divorce, look to find solutions to prevent the divorce and to achieve a happy marriage for both you and your children. To be sure you have the qualities required and can perform a real, happy marriage, if both of you cooperate sincerely, if you are both more tolerant with each other, if you make all the compromises necessary, if you do not worry about all kinds of complexes, if you want to understand the other, if you lose pride to nonsense, if you do what is necessary for both spouses and children to be happy and there is no need to do something the other does not desire, but what the situation requires to have a happy marriage. Trust in yourselves, you do not play with your marriage, your children, with your happiness because you have the qualities necessary to have a happy marriage and happy children and to surpass all the difficulties that appear.

2222. The qualities of the wife make the husband happy.

2223. The qualities of parents make children happy.

Respect

2224. They deserve to be appreciated, honored, respected and rewarded, all those journalists who do not act by order to unjustly hit some people, or groups of people.

2225. The correct behavior of a man towards his wife and other members of his family makes that man be very respected by his wife and members of his family.

2226. If we respect principles we will be more respected.

2227. Respecting principles helps us maintain true friendships.

2228. Prominent people must be respected for the good they do for mankind.

2229. Unfortunately in most of the world states there are still illegal court orders that do not respect human rights.

2230. Our life has been given to us so that we live it, but not in any way, mocking it, at chance, but thoughtly, economisingly, planningly, with good sense, with hopes, with positive thoughts and actions, with humanities, with love, with dedication only with what does us and others good. Good luck.

2231. You will succeed if you respect what there is to be respected, what you very well know and what must be respected. Good luck again.

2232. Fatigue can be prevented through the proper nutrition of the person concerned, through education, positive behavior, balanced life, intellectual exercises, perseverance, willpower, exercise, a value system that we believe in and that we respect, business dynamism, social relations, friends, mature love, a happy marriage, adequate rest when necessary, proper sleep, entertainment, etc..

2233. Self control must always be promoted, sustained, appreciated, respected and rewarded.

2234. Work must always be promoted, sustained, appreciated, respected and rewarded.

2235. Independence must always be promoted, appreciated, respected and rewarded.

2236. The sense of responsibility needs to be appreciated, promoted, supported and respected.

2237. Men must respect women who earn more than they do.

2238. People need and must act to sue all the elected and dignitaries, public clerks who do not respect their rights, who created damages.

2239. Honor must be promoted, supported, appreciated, respected and rewarded.

Biography

Gheorghe Cornel Ardelean was born on March 11.1954 in place Macea, Arad Country Romania Graduate of Economic University, Craiova Romania

1979-1989 Economist and Chief Economist and sales Department

In 1990-founding member of the first Parliament of Romania after the Revolution of 1989 in PCNU (Provisional Council of National Unity)

1992 - Independent candidate for deputy in the Romanian Parliament, Chamber of Deputies

1992-1996 Advisor to the Arad Country Council as an independent adviser

1992-1996 President of the Commission trade, tourism, services advise Arad Country Council

1990-2002 Director, manager of private companies wholesale

1980 - Philosopher and author books.

1980 He published 118 books, articles in publications, of which 50 English books and 68 books in Romanian

In 2009 - Member and Coordinator of Department programs, projects and activities of the non-profit. International Organisation Cornel Gheorghe Ardelean (OIAGC)

As a thought on long-term, positive, constructive, open, creative, humanistic, etc. It has a great ability to create so many positive ideas and solutions, constructive, humanist, creative, helpful people to achieve what they want. Thinking and ideas sustain and promote the rights of children, women, all people in the world, positive thinking and ideas, constructive, humanistic, tolerante, progressive, understanding and peace between peoples and nations.

www.ingramcontent.com/pod-product-compliance
Lightning Source LLC
Chambersburg PA
CBHW070831310526
45788CB00017B/91